HIBBERT LECTURES

THE
PHILOSOPHICAL BASES
OF THEISM

AMS PRESS

NEW YORK

Library of Congress Cataloging in Publication Data

Hicks, George Dawes, 1862-1941.
  The philosophical bases of theism.

  Reprint of the 1937 ed. which was published by
G. Allen & Unwin, London, in the series: Hibbert
lectures, 1931.
  Includes index.
  1. Theism.   2. God—Knowableness.   3. Philosophy
and religion.   4. Experience (Religion)   I. Title.
II. Series: Hibbert lectures; 1931.
BL200.H5   1979   211'.3   77-27142
ISBN 0-404-60427-7

First AMS edition published in 1979.

Reprinted from the edition of 1937, London. [Trim size and text
area of the original have been slightly altered in this edition.
Original trim size: 13.5 × 21.7 cm; text area: 9.3 × 16.2 cm.]

Hibbert Lectures

THE
PHILOSOPHICAL BASES
OF THEISM

by

G. DAWES HICKS

M.A., PH.D., LITT.D.

*Fellow of the British Academy and Emeritus Professor
of Philosophy in the University of London*

LONDON

GEORGE ALLEN & UNWIN LTD

MUSEUM STREET

FIRST PUBLISHED IN 1937

PRINTED IN GREAT BRITAIN BY
UNWIN BROTHERS LTD., WOKING

TO THE

MEMORY OF MY WIFE

LUCY KATHARINE DAWES HICKS,

AND OF HER UNFAILING HELP AND ENCOURAGEMENT

IN ALL MY WORK

PREFACE

THE substance of this book was delivered as Hibbert Lectures in the autumn of 1931 at University College, London, and at the University of Manchester. I have, however, revised and expanded the lectures as originally given in order to render the volume a somewhat more adequate treatment of the subjects with which it deals. Unhappily, partly through a protracted period of illness, and partly on account of a series of personal calamities, unavoidable delay has been occasioned in preparing the work for the press. I greatly regret the delay, and can only console myself with the reflexion that the line of thought I was following has in no wise become obsolete by the lapse of time.

These pages are designed primarily for the 'general reader'; and, accordingly, I have deliberately preserved the form of direct address appropriate in oral utterances and an essentially unconventional manner of handling the subject-matter. This has entailed that numerous repetitions will be met with which were almost inevitable in addresses to a popular and a partially fluctuating audience. I must apologize for these appearing in a printed volume, and venture to express the hope that they will not be found obtrusive.

I have been sustained throughout by the conviction that for those who have abandoned the resort of basing their religious trust on a miraculously attested revelation the philosophical approach to religion is indispensable, and is becoming increasingly seen to be so. I do not, by any means, desire to lend any countenance to the contention of Benedetto Croce and his Italian followers, that, namely, religion is an imperfect and immature attempt to interpret reality; and must, therefore, when once mythological notions have been discarded, yield its place to philosophy. On the contrary, theirs appears to me to be an entirely mistaken view of the nature both of religion and of philosophy. Nevertheless, whoever refuses to accept an external warrant, such as an infallible church or divinely inspired scriptures, has no alternative but to turn to the method of free rational inquiry, which in its more developed stage is the method of philosophy. For, although philosophy can as little provide us with a new religion as the science of ethics can provide us with a new morality, yet a religious mind that understands itself, that has reflected on the principles on which its religion rests, is clearly an advance upon the religious mind that has not so reflected. Without such reflexion, insistence upon the right or duty of private judgment is apt to result in a state of ennui and indifference. That is a danger which, as it seems to me, is threatening the liberal religious movement of the present age. Its crying need is for philosophic thinkers, not indeed to offer a substitute for religion, but to induce their fellows to interpret the facts of religious experience for themselves, in the light of critical scrutiny.

In preparing these lectures, I have had, then, specially in view the large number of persons who find themselves unable to accept the creeds of Christendom as they are familiarly presented, and who yet are persuaded that the spiritual life is a reality, and that they largely owe their sense of its reality to the teaching of Christ and the Christian Church. Obviously, to cover in the course of a few lectures the whole province of a philosophy of religion was out of the question. I could but select certain themes that appeared to me of crucial importance. In particular, I have had to leave on one side the great subject of human immortality, and the problem of evil, more especially the presence of physical evil in the natural world. With the former of these topics I have, however, dealt in the Essex Hall Lecture of 1934 and elsewhere; and with the latter I may perhaps still have occasion to deal later.

I gladly avail myself of this opportunity of giving expression to my deep sense of manifold indebtedness to the Hibbert Trustees. As a young man I was privileged, through holding one of their scholarships, to spend four most profitable years (1892–6) in the University of Leipzig, studying under such distinguished teachers as Wundt and Heinze. Later, in 1901, the Trustees received in an extremely kind and sympathetic manner a project I then, greatly daring, laid before them for the institution of a quarterly review which would be open to contributions from adherents to all schools of thought, and which ultimately led, in the following year, to the establishment of the *Hibbert Journal*, in the conduct of which I have since been permitted to play a humble part. And now, finally, I have to acknowledge, with sincere gratitude, the honour they did me in inviting me to give the present course of lectures, and thus to follow in the long line of eminent men who have preceded me as Hibbert Lecturers. And my gratitude is enhanced by the patience and the forbearance which the Trustees have shown during the delay in preparing this volume for the press.

G. DAWES HICKS

January 1937

CONTENTS

THE PHILOSOPHICAL BASES
OF THEISM

I

RELIGION AND PHILOSOPHY

1. Philosophy, an Interpretation of Experience in its entirety. 2. The term 'Experience' and its Meaning in this context. 3. Two considerations in regard to 'Experience'. 4. Relation of Philosophy to other departments of Knowledge. Sense in which it deals with ultimate problems. 5. Religious Experience and its influence in human history. 6. Need for a Philosophy of Religion.

THERE is a recorded saying of Goethe's to the effect that "the Christian religion has nothing to do with philosophy". The Christian religion, so Goethe went on to affirm, "is a mighty power in itself, whereby fallen and suffering humanity has from time to time constantly worked its way upwards; and, in so far as this is its outcome, it is elevated above all philosophy and does not need its support". In the sense in which he clearly meant this statement to be understood, Goethe was assuredly right. Certainly it cannot be said to have been as a result of philosophical reflexion that the Christian or any other religion either arose or has succeeded in exerting influence upon human thought. Relatively few of the religious leaders whose names stand out prominently in the pages of history have been philosophers, in the technical significance of the term. Rather has it been out of the great school of human experience that ideas such as those of the

Fatherhood of God, the brotherhood of men, the Incarnation, and of a continuance of life beyond the grave, have emerged; and in that school these ideas have been tried and tested prior to any direction upon them of logical scrutiny.

1. Nevertheless, regarded from a point of view other than that from which Goethe was here regarding it, it would obviously be ridiculous to assert that religion has nothing to do with philosophy, and does not need its support. While it is a notorious fact that countless persons for whom philosophy is a mere name may be and are intensely religious, yet those religious persons who have come, in whatsoever way, to think more or less philosophically—and their number is rapidly increasing—cannot fail to have their outlook on the whole field of religious experience affected thereby. A man may enter on the quest of philosophic truth, or he may abstain from doing so; but, if he does enter on it, and so far as he enters on it, he should be prepared to find that it will modify, if not radically transform, his views on all the deeper interests of human life.[1] Or, looking at the matter from the opposite side, though a religious mind may leave philosophy alone, the philosophic inquirer cannot leave religion alone. It is the business of philosophy to interpret, so far as may be, the world of human experience in its entirety; and were any

[1] A well-known disciple of Ritschl, W. Hermann, has, indeed, maintained that a man's faith can remain impregnable whatever his philosophy may be. Be he a materialist or an idealist in philosophy, his assurance of the validity of his religious convictions can continue unshaken. One can, I think, only express amazement at the *naïveté* of such a contention.

considerable sphere of that experience excluded from its survey, philosophic investigation would be frustrated *ab initio*. A man's philosophy, if he has any, cannot be other than all-embracing, all-penetrating. To refuse to allow his philosophy to interfere with his religious convictions "would signify only that he had not *thought through* his conception of things, that he had been contented with a partial glimpse, that his strength had flagged or his spirit failed in the heavy task of co-ordinating and systematically uniting his interpretations of the meaning of existence".

2. But to describe philosophy as the systematic expression of our reflexion on the nature and connectedness of experience is not in itself very enlightening. For 'experience' is a vague and ambiguous term, and not seldom it is apt to be employed after the manner of a conjuror's cry. It will be sufficient for our present purpose to differentiate three of the more common senses in which the term is used.

(*a*) When we say we know a thing by experience we frequently mean that instead of learning about it from others, instead of getting at it through words and general notions, we have been in direct contact with it. In actually seeing or hearing or touching it, we should be said to be more intimately acquainted with its being and character than we could possibly become by following any description of it, or merely thinking about it. Experience, so understood, is taken to arise through contacts with the things around us, much as a match strikes fire through friction and lights up what was dark before. Experience, that is to say, is regarded as the outcome of our active participation in the things of our environment[1]; and the contrast implied is that between what we directly apprehend, mainly, of course, through the avenue of sense-perception, and what we know, or believe that we know, through ordinary common-sense reasoning and logical inference.

(*b*) Again, in a somewhat more explicit manner, experience may be distinguished from science or strictly reasoned knowledge. And here the contrast chiefly turns upon the difference between knowledge of particular things or events and knowledge of truths or universal principles. This contrast carries us back to the great period of Greek philosophy. All human knowledge, so Aristotle maintained, starts with "the particulars"; it is, in other words, at the beginning, perception of individual objects. Then, through the aid of memory, crude generalities come to recognition; and these render possible what Aristotle called 'experience' (ἐμπειρία),—that common-sense knowledge which is adequate to discerning any single object as an instance or specimen of a kind or class already named by us. It is, he held, only by induction, which presupposes experience, that we reach the universal principles (τὰ καθόλου) on which scientific knowledge (ἐπιστήμη) is based, and thus come to an insight into the grounds or reasons of things. In experience, conceived in this way, the knowing mind is oblivious, so to speak, of its limitations and shortcomings.

But (*c*), when we appeal to experience, we may be

[1] "Experience", James Ward was fond of saying, "means becoming expert by experiment."

appealing to a recognition not so much of isolated facts or occurrences as to that of a context or system of facts or occurrences. By the term 'experience' there is then implied a unification of observations, —putting them, namely, together, comparing them, and consequently deriving a meaning out of them. When we speak of 'experience' in this wide sense we are obviously speaking of something in the formation of which the human mind has had a prominent part; an individual's experience, in this sense, will largely depend upon the manner of man he is. We shall only see, only experience, that which we bring with us the power of seeing or experiencing. Clearly also, when thus conceived, experience cannot be contrasted with knowledge or ἐπιστήμη. Rather does it embrace the latter along with much else besides. We distinguish, for example, scientific experience, moral experience, and aesthetic experience; or, in other words, we group what we experience under the three great ideas,—the true, the good, and the beautiful. And the question is at once suggested: What is implied in our mental constitution that these ideas should be possible for us? How come they to play the part they do in the experience of mature minds?

It is needful to note further that psychologists rightly lay stress upon the difference between the way in which an object is experienced and the way in which a mode of consciousness is experienced. We 'live through' (*erleben*) the latter, whereas the former is apprehended as standing over against us (as a *Gegenstand*). We may have experience of a delightful locality; but we cannot experience it as we experience a pleasurable or painful emotion. We may have experience of the affection of a friend; but we cannot experience it after the manner in which we experience the affection we ourselves feel towards our friend.

The difference just indicated, which has been likened to the sort of difference drawn by grammarians between the objective and the cognate accusative, or, as has also been aptly suggested, to the difference between jumping a ditch and jumping a jump, is one which, as we shall see, is of considerable importance as bearing upon some of the issues that will call to be discussed. But, meanwhile, I would lay stress upon the fact that in the actual life of a human being these two modes of experiencing never occur in isolation; awareness of self and awareness of what is other than self are strictly correlative, and, so far as our knowledge extends, we are justified in saying that the one would be impossible apart from the other. Our experience implies, therefore, what has been described as the duality in unity of subject and object. It is invariably experience *of* something; it is not, that is to say, a self-subsisting entity, consisting merely of specific contents. It presupposes, on the one hand, an experiencing mind, capable of discriminating and recognizing both its own subjective modes of activity and features in the objective realm; and, on the other hand, a world of concrete facts, let us for the moment name it, the features of which are discernible and possessed of significance. Now, when philosophy is said to be "just the systematic expression of our reflexion on the nature and connectedness of experi-

ence", it is, of course, human experience in the
widest sense that is thereby intended,—the experience
of what is external no less than of what is internal,
the experience of moral ideals no less than of the
aspiration to 'realize' them, the experience commonly
called 'spiritual' no less than that which pertains to
sense. Whilst not ignoring the experience of primitive
minds, it is essentially with the experience of man's
maturity that philosophy has to do. And this experience
is throughout suffused with the thoughts and ideas,
the hopes and endeavours, the joys and griefs, of
untold generations of human beings. Embedded in
it, so to speak, are the concepts of natural science,
the revelations of artistic genius, the assurances and
trusts of religion.

3. It will be well to emphasize here certain other
considerations respecting the nature of experience.

In the first place, it is to be observed that even
the sense-experience of ordinary individuals is, as a
matter of fact, saturated with thoughts and meanings,
which are not, of course, themselves offered through
the avenue of the senses. It has become customary
to distinguish roughly, in the perception of an external
thing, two sets of factors, falling under the heads of
the 'given' and the interpretation which is put upon
what is 'given'. The interpretation consists largely,
in all cases, of notions or concepts that connect the
'given' with something previously apprehended, or
taken to be identical in character with it. When a new
object comes before us, it is at once interpreted in
accordance with some relation in which we think it
stands to what has been already cognized by us.

Careful inspection of the situation will, however, make manifest the excessive difficulty, if not the impossibility, of fixing upon any portion of the perceived whole as that which is immediately 'given', in contrast to the rest which is suggested or inferred. I hear, for example, a sound, and I at once recognize that it is the strike of the clock on the mantelpiece of my room. Or, I see through the window a green patch, and I at once perceive the tennis-court on the other side of the road. The so-called sense-data of every such perceptual situation are, that is to say, so indissolubly blended with meanings and interpretations that the attempt to separate them out and to view them as alone the elements which are directly 'given' and intuitively grasped evinces itself as a hopeless undertaking. I am not, for a moment, implying that the interpretations are mere phantasies woven by the mind and thrown out as a kind of ghostly clothing over the sensuous data. On the contrary, I should affirm that what I hear *is* the striking of the clock, that what I see *is* the tennis-court. But the point is that in thus hearing and seeing, I am not merely receptive of what is supposed to be immediately 'given'; I am all the while thinking, judging, interpreting; and, in doing so, am obtaining an incomparably more adequate knowledge of my actual surroundings than purely given sense-qualities could conceivably yield. Even assuming that bare sense-data are, so to speak, nature's first offerings to us, it is very evident that nature does not thereby disclose to us her real character, or, indeed, supply us with elements that in themselves could build up an experience of any kind. And, certainly, it is only for a thinking, rational mind that there is possible not alone a scientific view of the world, but such a view of it as an ordinary, common-sense intelligence possesses.

In the second place, experience, whether it be that of the individual or of the community—what James Ward named 'universal experience',—is perpetually undergoing change and development; and the development, while in some respects analogous to evolution in the animal kingdom, is, in other respects, unique in character. It resembles biological evolution in being a mode of advance which involves both differentiation and integration,—that is to say, while it is a movement towards increasing multiplicity and complexity, it remains, at the same time, a unity which holds its elements together even in their extremest diversity. But the terms 'complex' and 'simple' are seldom free from ambiguity; and what they mean in any particular context can scarcely be discovered otherwise than by considering the context itself. In the present case, it is certainly erroneous to suppose, as the older psychologists did, that those phases of experience which are the less developed, and which, on that account, may be described as the more simple, exhibit a simplicity of ultimate elements which, as development proceeds, enter merely into more and more complicated combinations. What, on the contrary, does characterize the earlier stages of experience is specially want of definiteness, want of precision, in the apprehension of relations among the contents discriminated. And these contents themselves appear as relatively vague and obscure, lacking sharpness of outline and loosely connected with one another. "The steel-worker sees half a dozen tints where others see only a uniform glow." Advancing experience is, so to speak, like a pattern gradually coming out; and, in its later phases, as contrasted with the earlier, the contents experienced are characterized by the constantly increasing number of the points of difference which the experiencing subject recognizes, by an increase of closeness in the relations whereby the several features are grouped together, and by a change in the character of the relations through which they are connected. Yet there is no violent break between one such phase and another; at every stage of transition, there is a certain whole of experience which is one and continuous, and advance comes about not by the abrupt introduction of what is altogether new, but by a partial modification of what has preceded. Moreover, so far as the experiencing subject is concerned, development means not the emergence of new psychical powers or faculties. Speaking generally, in the more developed stages of conscious activity there is nothing which is not generically akin to that which enters into the simpler forms.

4. These, then, are characteristic features of experience in that sense of the term in which philosophy may be said to be an attempt to explicate, and to render intelligible, experience as a whole. But the function of philosophy may be contemplated from various points of view; and I wish now to glance briefly at two ways of regarding it which have been prominent in the history of thought.

Philosophy, so many of its greatest devotees have

held, has for its subject-matter the nature of *ultimate* reality. In Platonism, for example, the conception of philosophy turned essentially upon a profound difference, amounting almost to a decided opposition, between the things of ordinary experience and entities or essences (ἰδέαι or εἴδη) which were thought to possess a superior kind of being. The things of ordinary experience bore the marks of an inferior or deficient grade of reality, in that they are always changing, transient and perishable, and hence had no definite, specific nature; the eternal essences, on the other hand, bore the countermarks of fixity and permanence. And, as regards the knowledge we may obtain of these two contrasted realms of being, it too must obviously display difference of a corresponding kind. Of the variable and the fleeting there could be no knowledge in the strict sense (ἐπιστήμη); there could, at the most, be knowledge merely of that inferior grade designated belief or opinion (δόξα). Only in respect of what is fixed and permanent could knowledge attain its full dimensions, and possess the character of necessary and eternal truth. Furthermore, all those branches of research which we are now in the habit of describing as the natural sciences, seeing that they have to do with the variable and the changing, must clearly, on this view, be looked upon as falling within the sphere of belief or opinion. Consequently, a difference of kind called to be recognized as subsisting between ordinary experience, with its outcome the natural sciences, and philosophical thinking; the objects thought about were different, the kinds of thinking in the two cases were different.

Now, a sharp and rigid separation of this sort between two portions of our experience cannot but prove fatal to the possibility of reaching any coherent view of the system of things. Such a separation may doubtless be looked upon as an exaggeration of a distinction among the elements of experience that does call for recognition; but in philosophy no error is more common than that of taking a half-truth to be the whole truth. When, in the modern period, the special sciences had attained a measure of independence, another (which may, perhaps, be designated the Cartesian) way of contemplating the function of philosophy became prevalent. This would appear, on the surface, at least, to steer clear of that 'bifurcation' of experience to which I have been alluding, and to draw no hard and fast line of demarcation between philosophical thinking and scientific thinking. According to it, philosophic thinking may be said to be the culminating, the ultimate, stage of advance on ordinary or common-sense thinking. The last mentioned, the lowest grade, is first of all transcended by the special sciences, in each of which general principles are formulated that to a certain extent explain vast numbers of individual facts. The attempt to proceed further *in the same direction*, the attempt to elucidate and to justify these principles employed in the special sciences, leads to philosophy. Philosophy would, therefore, be said to be distinguished from the special sciences, on the one hand, by the greater generality of its fundamental concepts, and, on the other hand, by the ultimate character of its problems and of the solution it furnishes of those problems.

It has thus become customary to represent philosophy as the effort to obtain a conception of the complete or absolute nature of reality.

The terms 'ultimate' and 'absolute', even when safeguarded, have, however, their dangers. If understood in one way, they are liable to reinstate the antithesis which proved to be the *impasse* before which Platonism was brought to a stand. The 'Absolute' will be pictured as that which is somehow quite other than, quite remote from, the relative and the particular. Nevertheless, I believe that there is ground for attributing an ultimate character, if understood in another way, to the problems of philosophy. But the ultimate character which *does* belong to them is due, it seems to me, to the circumstance that in what we call philosophical reflexion all the parts of what we take to be reality, be they many or be they few, are contemplated as having a common relation. They are contemplated, namely, in their relation to the thoughts and interests of the human conscious subject. There is, that is to say, no one group of entities which is specifically the subject-matter of philosophy, nor is there one type of explanation which is specifically *the* philosophical type of explanation. Any part or the whole of experience may be handled philosophically if treated from the point of view of its relation to the human thinking subject. So, again, it will be apparent that philosophy, when so regarded, may be said to have, in one sense, a subject-matter of its own, a subject-matter which is not dealt with by any of the natural sciences, because each of these necessarily leaves out of account the unique relation just referred to.[1] And, once more, it will likewise be apparent that philosophical reflexion, although not a different kind of thinking from scientific thinking, has its own peculiar nature in virtue of the special end to which it is directed and the special relation on which it turns. In short, philosophy has one main comprehensive question addressed to it: What light can it throw on the relation in which the human mind stands to the surrounding reality? What must the character of reality be, if it admits of being known, and what must be the nature of the intelligence that is capable of knowing it?

The subordinate branches of philosophical inquiry will be obviously determined by the main differences that can broadly be distinguished in the relation which subsists between the human mind and the surrounding reality. Long ago, Aristotle classified these differences under three heads,—namely, the relation involved in knowledge, the relation involved in practical conduct, and the relation involved in artistic production.[2] It requires, however, but little consideration to see that of these three types of relation the first is by far the more fundamental. Whilst practical activity and artistic activity are certainly distinguishable from cognitive activity, yet they both imply the latter as the very condition of their possibility. It has not seldom been contended that individual experience

[1] It may be objected that psychology furnishes an exception to this statement. But I should contend that, in tracing the history of the mental life and in determining the conditions on which it depends, psychology is essentially a branch of philosophy.

[2] To these, had he been living some centuries later, Aristotle would probably have added the relation involved in religious experience.

is primarily conative in character, and gradually becomes cognitive because knowing proves subservient to action. But, unless conative activity were based on some degree of knowledge, it could not occur at all; the most that could happen would be particular automatic movements of which the conscious subject would be unaware. And it is not merely that in conative activity we first know and then act; the knowing goes on throughout the act. In fact, it may be asserted unreservedly that the human mind depends for its very being upon its capacity of knowing; it is only in and through the process of knowing that it has a place in the scheme of existence.

"Experience", James Ward was fond of insisting, "is wider than knowledge." Yes; but it is no less true that there can be no experience without knowledge.[1] Experience is not, as we have seen, a self-subsisting entity; it is only in virtue of knowing minds, which are also centres of feeling and striving, being face to face, so to speak, with a natural environment that experience comes into being. So far, then, from conscious minds being owned, as F. H. Bradley conceived, by experience, the fact rather is that experience is owned by conscious minds, if, indeed, it is permissible in this context to talk of 'ownership' at all. And, on the other hand, it has to be remembered that a mind is not a mere abstraction, that it exists only in and through its concrete modes of expression,

[1] The term "knowing" is, it need hardly be said, equivocal. But one may be allowed here to use the term in its widest sense, as equivalent, namely, to cognizing generally.

through participating, that is to say, in the reality of what is other than itself.

Enough has been said to indicate the kind of inquiries which the philosophic investigator has before him in dealing with experience. In the first place, since knowing, as distinguished from what is known, is obviously a subjective process, there is always the possibility that this subjective process may fail to reach what would seem to be its natural end, the attainment, namely, of truth. In the second place, since experience—whether individual experience or common experience—is gradually acquired, clearly it cannot at all stages of its history be equally accurate, let alone exhaustive, experience of the real world. I have, indeed, maintained that the development of experience does not involve that the experiencing mind becomes, at certain junctures in its progress, endowed with absolutely new powers or faculties, but that, on the contrary, the higher operations of intelligence are not, in essential characteristics, distinct from the lower. While, then, experience of the cruder sort is relatively circumscribed and defective, it is not necessarily, on that account, thoroughly deceptive and illusory. Though Nature could not touch the heart of Peter Bell—

> "By lovely forms, and silent weather,
>   And tender sounds, yet you might see
>   At once, that Peter Bell and she
>   Had often been together."

Nevertheless, there is manifestly a tremendous difference between the extent to which the earlier phases of experience correspond to actual fact and the extent to which the later phases do. And these two considerations—(*a*) that the subjective process of cognizing or experiencing is liable to fall into error, and (*b*) that what we call knowledge or experience is, in the course of its history, continually undergoing correction, expansion, and deepening, indicate at once the necessity of determining the conditions to which thought or thinking,—instrumental, as it is, in the building up of experience,—must conform, if we are to be reasonably assured that what we are thereby attaining is true, holds good, that is, for every intelligence, or, otherwise expressed, is objectively valid. And this critical examination of experience leads inevitably to what may be designated the culminating aim of philosophical or metaphysical inquiry, to reach, namely, such a conception of the world of reality as will render intelligible the attainment of truth by human thinking, as also the conjoined operation of mental and physical processes in nature. The ultimate task of philosophy must always be to frame a coherent representation of reality as a whole, a representation which will enable us to connect together consistently and harmoniously the several parts and aspects of our total experience.

5. On the far-reaching influence of religious thought and sentiment in human experience, as we have been viewing it, I need not dwell. Religion is from the first, so Hegel once remarked, the bearer (*Träger*) of human culture. What, then, does this comprehensive term, religion, really signify? An exhaustive answer could only be obtained from an

adequate survey of the manifold modes of manifestation of that which is so named in the course of the history of mankind. To attempt to reach a verbal definition, which should set forth the characteristic common to all types of religious belief, is for the purpose of a philosophical treatment, at any rate, a perfectly futile undertaking. In the first place, it is more than doubtful whether any such common characteristic is to be found. At all events, the various and conflicting formulations of it which have from time to time been framed are, to say the least, sufficient to restrain further endeavours in that direction. In the second place, such a common characteristic, even if it could be detected, would be of so vague and so colourless a nature as to be virtually destitute of any real significance. What can be made, for instance, of so general and abstract an assertion as that "religion is man's total response to his *entire* realized universe"? And, in the third place, such a common characteristic would have to be sought in religions of the most primitive and superstitious kinds; by thus reducing religion to its lowest terms, we should be losing its essence and grasping its wrappings. When, for example, Sir James Frazer defines religion as "a propitiation or conciliation of powers superior to man which are believed to direct and control the course of nature and of human life",[1] one is at a loss to understand how, according to such a definition, Christianity can be supposed to be a religion at all.

The fact is that a procedure of this sort is, as Edward Caird and others have convincingly shown, utterly

[1] *The Golden Bough*, 3rd ed., vol. i, p. 222.

out of place in dealing with anything which, like
religion, has been, down the ages, undergoing continuous evolution. With respect to whatsoever grows
and develops, it is the higher stages that help us to
understand and to gauge aright that which is evinced
in the lower. No examination, be it ever so minute,
of the seed or embryo would enable us to predict
what it will in the course of time become, unless we
were already familiar with the distinctive lineaments
of the full-grown plant or animal. Then, doubtless,
when we trace back the mature organism to the germ
from which it sprang, a study of the process of genesis
throws a flood of light upon the nature of that which
has ultimately emerged. But the point is that "in the
first instance, at least, we must read development
backward and not *forward*, we must find the key to
the meaning of the first stage in the last". What,
therefore, we have to look for is not a characteristic
common to every type of religion, but rather "a
germinative principle", as it has been called, underlying all types, "a motive power, working in the
human mind, and essentially bound up with its
structure". It is in their relation to this underlying
principle, and not in any doctrines or external features
which they possess in common, that religions have
their basis of agreement. To a large extent the history
of religious beliefs is, indeed, the exhibition of the
constant conflict between the imperfections of the
concrete imagery which the human mind calls to its
aid in representing what it takes to be divine reality
and the demands of the fundamental principle which
that imagery obscurely embodies, a conflict in and

through which the full significance of the principle itself gradually comes to recognition. The history of religions may, then, be said to be just religion progressively defining itself; and a clear discernment of its essence will be obtained, not by "peering into its cradle and seeking oracles in its infant cries", but by contemplating it in the more mature forms to which it has attained as the outcome of the entire process of its development. And no one, I take it, would seriously dispute the statement that the whole trend of the evolution in question has been towards a belief in God as one and not as many, manifesting Himself both in nature and to the mind of man, yet revealing Himself most completely to souls of large spiritual compass and of strenuous moral power.

I am not, it need hardly be said, intending to suggest that in the history of religions we invariably encounter continuous, uninterrupted progress. Far from it. Such a contention would notoriously be contrary to fact. Repeatedly, in a period of great spiritual vitality and fervour, a large expansive religious movement has carried all before it; and then gradually the spiritual activities seem to wane and lose their power, and a period of stagnation to supervene. The life of that movement may not, it is true, have fled; it may only for a while be lying dormant, ready at a later time and under favourable conditions to issue forth in new forms of growth. Or, it may be that it proves itself to be incapable of further development in keeping with the developing life of mankind. Perchance, under the influence of stereotyped forms of creed and ritual, it has become rigid and mechanical,

and hence resists the internal reconstruction that
would bring it into harmony with the advancing
thought and aspirations of the age. Its life then ebbs
away, and decadence ensues. But, even so, it does
not follow that what once was living and good therein
will be lost to posterity. St. Paul told the Athenians
that what they had been worshipping in ignorance,
this he was setting forth unto them; and certain is
it that had Christianity not been able to appropriate,
transmute, and so to preserve much at least that was
valuable in Greek and Roman religion it would not
be the power it is in the world to-day.

Without assuming, then, a continuous linear progress from the lowest to the highest, or attempting
to trace, after the manner of Hegel, a necessary
dialectical movement in the temporal development
of religious systems, it can unhesitatingly be asserted
that an impartial survey of the historical data leads
unmistakably to the conclusion that advance on the
whole there unquestionably has been to ever purer
and loftier conceptions of God and of God's relation
to the world. Moreover, although, of course, the *con-
sensus gentium* is no guarantee of validity, although
an *Athanasius contra mundum* may veritably be in
possession of a discernment to which the *Millionen*
cannot attain, yet an impressive fact certainly it is,
and a fact not lightly to be discounted, that in every
known period of history some kind of religious beliefs
and religious observances have been in evidence, in
tribes and nationalities the most unlike in other
respects, too remote from one another to allow the
possibility of mutual influence, and pursuing the

most divergent lines of practical activity. This fact would seem to be, at any rate, sufficient to justify the assumption that religion is native to man, not a product of arbitrary or capricious surmisings, but a normal and universal expression of human nature.

There are, it is true, some writers at the present day who look upon the religious ideas of the modern world as mere superstitions or survivals of ancient beliefs, which arose originally in pre-historic times, and which through various causes have been perpetuated, in modified and refined form, to our age of scientific enlightenment. That would appear to be the view taken, for example, by a well-known philosophic thinker, in a work published only a few years ago.[1] He connects primitive animism in various ways with magic; and, regarding them both as being very much on the same level, sets himself the task of explaining how it comes about that the human mind is everywhere befogged with beliefs of this sort, whilst the anthropoids seem not to be troubled by them, but to live by common-sense. And his account of the matter is that these beliefs, baseless though they be and due entirely as they are to the sway of imagination unchecked by reflexion, are yet apt to become, in virtue of their utility, inextricably blended with common-sense, skill, and intelligence. These illusory notions have been useful; they have served to give elders and rulers enough prestige to preserve order and cohesion when otherwise they would have been lacking in authority. And, thus,

[1] Carveth Read, *The Origin of Man and of his Superstitions*, Cambridge: University Press, 1920.

"perverse as it may seem, imaginations utterly false have had their share in promoting 'progress'; co-operating with agriculture and trade, they have, by supporting government and civil order, helped in accommodating us, and even in some measure adapting us, to 'our present condition, such as it is'."[1]

But, even supposing that the whole trend of religious thought and feeling has been in the wrong direction, and that reliance on a Divine Being is destined some day to become extinct, this mode of explaining the facts can scarcely be pronounced plausible. 'Natural selection' must not, it is true, in such a context, be thought of as purposive; but why 'our present condition, such as it is', should be the outcome of 'natural selection' up to date, or why 'utility' should weight the scales in favour of fictitious fancies and illusions, it is hard to divine. I suppose that even those who take the view we are considering would admit that, so far as the evolution of human intelligence is concerned, a mode of thought which is in accordance with fact is more likely to survive than one which totally mis-represents it. If, then, religious belief owed its origin solely to the working of irrational phantasy, should we not naturally expect it to be local and partial in its operation, and the bias towards it in one region to be counteracted by the bias against it in another? Should we not naturally expect, also, to observe a tendency in human history to throw off so extraneous and so needless a load? Yet, so far from witnessing anything of the kind, what we actually *do* find is persistent and unabated effort on the part of many of

[1] Cf. Sir James Frazer's interesting volume, *Psyche's Task.*

our foremost intellects to frame worthier conceptions of that which is taken to be divine, and unwearied search for more adequate ways of expressing those conceptions. Indeed, it is no exaggeration to say that the finest products of human creativeness owe their very being and inspiration to religion. What would be left of the art of the last twenty centuries and more if all that were abstracted which symbolizes religious ideas and emotions? Pheidias helped to spiritualize the religion of Greece no less than Raphael the religion of Italy. From religion, too, literature has derived its sublimest themes, and the soul which makes it living. Take away from the minds of a Plato, a Dante, a Milton, a Goethe, a Wordsworth, or a Browning, their religious trust, and what would remain of their thought and genius? There must, then, surely be something strangely odd and perverse about the intelligence of man if its greatest achievements only come to fruition through means of crude superstitions and baseless dreams.[1]

A complaint not seldom to be heard in these days comes, however, from another quarter. Despite external appearances to the contrary, it is frequently urged, genuine faith in a living God is far less widespread now than it used to be in times gone by. Too often

[1] Furthermore, any theory which is compelled to fall back upon such vague generalities as 'natural selection', 'utility', 'imagination', and the like, in order to explain what would otherwise be for it utterly inexplicable, at once awakens suspicion. I, for one, am convinced that occult agencies such as these, which even in this scientific age are being perpetually summoned from the vasty deep, will come by posterity to be regarded very much as we now regard the magical potencies of pre-scientific ages. Superstitious survivals are constantly to be met with even in those circles that are most intent upon exorcizing them.

such faith has become little more than a tradition which it is respectable to acknowledge, but about which it is superfluous to be serious. As voicing this desponding thought, Dr. Martineau once wrote: "If to-morrow atheism were somehow to prove true, it would make a difference, like the explosion of a geologic theory, in our conception of the origin of worlds; but London and Paris would not feel it as they would the death of a statesman or a president. The future would lose a hope, the past a sacredness; but no passion of the hour would be changed, no instant sense of bereavement lay the city low."[1] That Dr. Martineau intended himself to endorse that judgment is, I think, unlikely[2]; but, in any case, one may venture to doubt whether the prediction here recorded is really warranted. London and Paris are, of course, thickly populated areas; and it is certainly the case that large numbers of their inhabitants, caught up as they are in the whirl of aimless pleasure-seeking, vegetate through life instead of humanly living it. And of such as these, it is doubtless true that reflexion is not a characteristic trait,—reflexion on the spiritual aspects of reality least of all. Nevertheless, a change of the kind indicated might well affect them far more closely than at first sight seems prob-

[1] *Hours of Thought*, vol. ii, pp. 220–21.

[2] "It is", Dr. Martineau writes elsewhere, "a pathetic thing to see how hard it is for a human soul to let its religion go; to watch how those who, from loss of the infinite Father, find themselves in an orphaned universe, would fain attempt compensation by worshipping either each other, or even, while its sacred look yet lingers, the mere scene where he was, and persuade themselves that it is still the same piety, though they stand alone and no one reads their heart or hears their orisons" (*Study of Religion*, vol. i, p. 11).

able. In a civilized community even shallow and insipid minds rely instinctively, as it were, for their security upon the thought and aspiration of others; the assurances of the devout form a sort of subconscious background of their inner being. They breathe and move in an atmosphere of theism; and, although they would themselves be the last to suspect it, transportation into an atmosphere of demonstrated atheism would mean, even for them, a privation hard to gauge. The miller who has become habituated to the sound of his wheel sleeps through the night undisturbed so long as the rhythmic sound continues, but no sooner does the wheel come suddenly to a stand than he is awakened by an undefined sense of void or feeling of uneasiness. The simile is not altogether inappropriate. When wiser souls were conscious of a desolate stillness in the realm of spiritual being, even moth-like devotees of frivolity would be turned, well-nigh unconsciously, into fellow mourners; and from the gloom into which humanity would then be plunged even they would find no means of escape.

The contingency hinted at in the passage I have cited need, however, occasion no forebodings. Huxley once observed that, of all the senseless babble he had ever come across, the arguments of those who undertake to tell us all about the nature of God would be the worst, if they were not surpassed by the still greater absurdities of those who try to prove that there is no God. And should the human race continue on this earth throughout the future ages during which astronomers anticipate it will be capable of sustaining life, a validly demonstrated atheism will not, it is safe to predict, be one of mankind's ultimate achievements.

From the point of view of history, little support can, then, be found for the view that the religion of modern civilization is but a superstitious and illusory form of consciousness, destined to be cast aside with the increase of scientific enlightenment. Rather, in that wonderful little tract of his, published in 1780, a year before his death, did Lessing gather up the main lessons to be gleaned from a survey of the historical development. Lessing's essay was extremely brief; and it was restricted almost entirely to a consideration of the relation between Judaism and Christianity. But it opened out great vistas of 'intellectual space', and it was replete with deep and penetrating thoughts, clothed in simple and persuasive language. Its central theme,—that of Revelation, not as ready-made and final truth, authoritative for all time and all people, but as a continuous process, advancing through successive steps, according to the progressive capacity of the human mind, and comparable to the process of education in the case of an individual personality,—was strikingly at variance with the principles both of the orthodox and rationalistic writers of the period, yet it proved to be fruitful beyond measure for those who, early in the nineteenth century, first mapped out the field of a philosophy of religion, in the sense in which that term is now understood. The suggestiveness of Lessing's treatment was principally due to the circumstance that it broke down the artificial barrier which had been erected between reason and revelation; and, by giving a wider scope to reason and a more rational meaning to revelation, made clear that any revelation of a Divine Being must be sought in the whole course of nature and of human history, as well as in the richest intellectual and spiritual experiences of individual souls.

6. In the period following that of Lessing, no less than now, the question has been pressed: Assuming revelation to be of the character indicated, what need is there for a philosophy of religion? If it be granted that the evidence for what the religious man takes to be indubitable truths is furnished in nature and human history, and above all in actual personal experience, then, surely, we have the same kind of warrant for them as we have for the existence of objects and persons in our immediate vicinity. He who is thus conscious of divine things at first hand requires not to justify his assurance by logical argument. They are there—these spiritual realities—and it is no less futile to seek proof of their being than to seek for proof of the being of the sun when it is shining in the sky. To a certain extent Lessing himself provided a sufficient answer to objections of this sort. Revelation, like culture generally, is, he insisted, in its very nature *progressive*; in its primitive forms, it must of necessity be intertwined with much that in the course of time will evince itself as made up of merely human accretions, and which will, with increasing insight, fall away. It is, for example, vain to complain that the Jehovah of the early Israelites was but a tribal deity; at that incipient stage of human culture, no higher conception of the one God could have been framed. If, even now, truth must be 'em-

bodied in a tale' that it may 'enter into lonely doors',
much more *then* was it inevitable that truth should
be viewed through limited apertures. The schoolboy
is taught that the square of three is nine, that nine
has three as its square root, and dimly understands,
perhaps, the sense of what he has learnt; but for the
mathematician this proposition has a meaning altogether beyond the schoolboy's ken. In fine, truth
imparted is never grasped as truth achieved is grasped;
and when the God of Israel was ultimately discerned
to be 'the high and lofty One that inhabiteth eternity'
the hard-won discovery possessed a significance richer
far than any dogma, dictated, say, to Moses on the
Mount, could conceivably have possessed. The
elaboration of revealed truths into truths of reason
must, so Lessing averred, be the aim and purpose of
the whole scheme of 'the education of the human
race'. "When they were revealed they were certainly
not yet truths of reason, but they were revealed in
order to become such."

This last statement must not, however, be mis-
understood. While emphatically rejecting the claim
that any one of the positive religions of the world
possessed a final revelation of God to be accepted,
without scrutiny or criticism, as infallible truth,
Lessing would most assuredly have resisted no less
unreservedly the view inculcated in these days by
Benedetto Croce that religion is but an immature
and inferior grade of philosophy, and destined when
stripped of its mythological elements to be transformed into philosophy pure and simple. Lessing, on
the contrary, would have been among the first to

acknowledge that philosophy can no more take the place of religious experience than ethics can take the place of moral experience, or aesthetics the place of artistic experience. He would have agreed that to construe religion is one thing, and to construct it quite another. As Hegel afterwards affirmed: "What philosophy has to do is to know religion as something which is actually in being. Neither its intention nor its office is it to induce this or that person to be religious if he has not been so before, if he has nothing of religion in him, and does not wish to have."

The function of philosophy in regard to religious experience is, in fact, very similar, in one respect, to its function in regard to sense-experience. We have noted that in sense-experience the merely 'given' factors, if such there be, constitute a relatively small portion of the content experienced, and that taken alone they would constitute no experience. It is essential that the cognitive activity of the individual experiencing subject should come into play, grasping or recognizing the revelations of sense, comparing and combining them, and interpreting them as features of some actual fact. And, if in religious experience there be revelations of a supersensuous kind, we can hardly conceive that *recognition* of them as such is also, along with them, communicated, or imported, so to speak, ready made into the mind without the operation on the individual's part of any process of intellection.[1] Rather are we constrained to acknowledge that such recognition must imply, as

---

[1] As is, in fact, practically asserted by many of those who claim to have had certain forms of mystical experience.

recognition in all other cases implies, the exercise of cognitive activity, that what is 'given' is only experienced as a revelation through the agency of reflexion, which discriminates its contents and interprets it by notions that are capable of being connected with those which we bring to bear upon our environment generally. However impressive and awe-inspiring an experience may have been, however persuaded the experient may be that what he experienced was a divine manifestation, still the conviction that it was so is *his* conviction; and, like every other conviction of his, not exempt from the possibility of error and illusion. The Greek sculptor who, on finishing a statue, fell on his knees before it, because he felt that its beauty was no mere creation of his own, but something heavenly, may have been justified in his belief, but no one would contend that it was beyond the range of doubt or question. Just, therefore, because the experient's own thought or reason is implicitly or explicitly involved in his interpretation of an experience as a divine revelation, that interpretation calls for the inspection and the scrutiny of critical reflexion. And when religion, on account of its sanctity, seeks to exempt itself from such critical scrutiny, it awakens, in Kant's memorable words, just suspicion, and cannot claim the sincere respect which reason accords only to that which has been able to sustain the test of free and open inquiry.

Furthermore, not only is it the function of philosophical criticism to scrutinize what are taken to be the contents of religious experience, and to differentiate, so far as may be, those which may be legitimately regarded as of real value from those which may not, there belongs also to it the function of analysing and of determining the significance of the notions familiarly employed in handling religious themes. In interpreting experience of any kind, ordinary thought makes use of a number of concepts—such as those of substance, change, cause, etc.—and uses them more or less consistently, yet usually without any clear or definite idea as to their meaning or implication. Now, especially in interpreting religious experience, the notions which ordinary thought has at its disposal must, by the very necessity of the case, be meagre and thoroughly inadequate. It is bound to express in pictorial and symbolic phraseology what otherwise it could not express at all. When, for instance, the Deity is spoken of as having eyes to behold the righteous, and ears open to their cry, when He is represented as being enthroned in some celestial locality, and as sending forth from thence emissaries to execute His designs, or as even Himself riding upon a cherub and flying swiftly upon the wings of the wind, no understanding person is misled by these metaphorical modes of expression. But even the more refined and elevated utterances of the religious consciousness labour more or less under the same disability. When the Divine Being is said to operate on human minds very much after the manner in which physical things operate on one another, or to make human minds His temple or dwelling-place, or to "breathe the eternal poem of the universe, and attune our minds to hear it", we recognize, once more, the symbolical character of these phrases, and that, though they may be sufficiently

adequate for the purpose of awakening devout medi-
tation and feeling, yet they would be manifestly
thoroughly inappropriate if taken to be exact equiva-
lents for spiritual truths. It is, then, the business of
critical reflexion to examine the notions thus figuratively
conveyed, to endeavour to bring out clearly their
essential meaning, and to ascertain how far the several
beliefs which they indicate are consistent with one
another.

A philosophy of religion is not, however, confined
to the work of critically examining notions of the
kind just indicated. The central affirmation of the
religious consciousness, at least in modern times,
is the proposition 'God exists'; and that proposition
raises at once the basal issues of any constructive
philosophy of religion. Religious conviction, in its
purest form, is the assurance of a conscious relation,
on our part, to a higher mind than ours; and, on the
part of human beings at large, to a higher than all,
or, in other words, to a supreme Mind transcending
the whole family of dependent minds. To that conviction the poet Schiller gave, for example, utterance in
tones of unfaltering confidence:

"Ein Gott ist, ein heiliger Wille lebt,
    Wie auch der menchliche wanke;
Hoch über der Zeit und dem Raume webt
    Lebendig der höchste Gedanke;
Und, ob Alles in ewigem Wechsel kreist,
Es beharret im Wechsel ein ruhiger Geist."

Can confidence such as this be rationally justified?
Have we reliable grounds for thinking that human

intellects are thus able to grasp that which would seem to be so far beyond the range of their limited powers of apprehension? And, if we have, what sort of knowledge is it? Does it involve apprehension of a unique kind, or is our knowing in this case akin to that which leads us to discernment of the ways of nature, and to acquaintance with the thoughts and actions of our fellow creatures? And further, assuming it can be shown that there is no reason for doubting the human mind to be capable of such knowledge, the question has still to be faced whether the real universe, so far as the disclosures of science have made its nature manifest to us, is so constituted as to be in accord with the affirmations of religion. In short, is a theistic conception consistent with such an interpretation of the whole of our experience, as philosophy is now in a position to offer? These, then, are the issues with which we shall be occupied in the succeeding lectures.

MAN'S PLACE IN NATURE

1. True and false Anthropomorphism. 2. The Limits of the theory of Evolution in its bearing upon the development of man as a rational being. 3. "Scientific Naturalism", its shortcomings as a Philosophy. 4. Positivism, a false Anthropomorphism.

1. IF what has been said in the last lecture concerning the character of philosophical inquiry be justified, the point of view of the philosopher must clearly be in one sense anthropomorphic, and the standpoint of a philosophy of religion particularly so. Yet this in no way entails that the results obtained from such an inquiry must be narrow or circumscribed. There is, it is true, a delusive and crude anthropomorphism, such as that which Locke was thinking, when he spoke of man "setting himself proudly at the top of all things". But there is likewise an anthropomorphism which is circumspect and enlightened. This latter emphasizes the consideration that the notions or concepts which we employ, in unravelling the facts of nature, are derived from human experience by means of our own reflective thought. And, although other planets may be inhabited by beings with sense-organs more numerous and more acute than ours, still knowledge or intellectual achievement, wherever it is to be met with, must be in essence one; there can be no means of knowing or interpreting the world other than that of thought or intelligence.

A sane anthropomorphism, even of the kind just

indicated, is, however, in these days apt to be discredited. So long as the old Jewish cosmology prevailed, there was no incongruity in picturing man as the crowning product of creation. The compact little cosmos, which had come into existence only a few thousand years before, of which the earth was the centre and the firmament that which divided the waters from the waters, and most of which imagination or thought could traverse by easy excursions, seemed framed on a scale suited to be the scene whereon the drama of human history was being enacted. In one of those superb passages, which prove him to have been one of the greatest religious geniuses of the world, St. Paul, for instance, represents so-called inanimate nature as a preparatory stage of the cosmic process which reaches its completion and its goal in the spiritual lives of the 'sons of God'. Physical nature was, he conceived, full of the promise and potency of that which is to be. It was, as he pictured it, an expectant, anticipatory creation; it evinced, he even ventured to suggest, a sort of dumb sympathy with the struggles and the successes and the failures of men.

The modern astronomer will not have it so. To him "it seems incredible that the universe can have been designed primarily to produce life like our own; had it been, we might have expected to find a better proportion between the magnitude of the mechanism and the amount of the product." The total number of stars at present existing is, we are told, something like the number of grains of sand on all the sea-shores of this planet; "such is the littleness of our home in space when measured up against the total substance of the universe". Moreover, life seems to him to be "an utterly unimportant by-product", and we living beings to be "somehow off the main lines". It was, indeed, an accident that brought this earth into being at all; some two thousand millions of years ago it happened that, along with the other planets of the solar system, it was drawn off from the sun by a gravitational pull of a passing star. Another accident was it that life originally made its appearance on the earth's surface; and the time will come when that life will meet an inglorious extinction.

It is, perhaps, worth noting that in one respect there is, in a sense, at least, a strange reversion on the part of the modern astronomer to the cosmology of the early Christian era. Until recently, since the days of Copernicus in fact, speculation had been rife in respect to countless other worlds than ours that might be inhabited by intelligent minds. At the present time, however, the conclusion rather is that, insignificant though this globe be in the scheme of things, its surface may nevertheless be the sole locality on which living creatures can exist, and that, in any case, life must be limited to corners of the universe, relatively speaking, amazingly small. But this conclusion tends rather, it is held, to confirm than to dispel the view that is being maintained. For the thought of the colossal scale of "the incomprehending masses of space", outside these "small corners", is sufficient of itself to discredit the idea that the furtherance of life "forms a special interest of the great Architect of the universe".

The outlook so depicted is calculated, no doubt,

to awaken in thoughtful minds a sense of misgiving
if not of despair. As thus portrayed the universe
wears unquestionably a terrifying look,—terrifying
because of its vast seemingly meaningless distances,
because of its inconceivably long vistas of time; and,
above all, because of its apparent indifference, if not
distinct hostility, to conscious natures such as ours.
Sir James Jeans, from whose booklet[1] I have been
quoting, seeks, it is true, in his concluding pages,
to mitigate the impression that we are strangers or
intruders in the realm of matter by contending that
quite recent science seems to be heading towards the
conception of a non-mechanical reality. "The universe", he here avers, "shows evidence of a designing
or controlling power that has something in common
with our own individual minds,—not, so far as we
have discovered, emotion, morality, or aesthetic
appreciation, but the tendency to think in the way
which, for want of a better word, we describe as
mathematical." Without, in the least, venturing to
call in question this rendering of the more recent
tendencies of physical research, I have to confess
that I do not see how it can be supposed appreciably
to alleviate the feeling of depression which Sir James
Jeans pictured so vividly at the beginning of his
work. The huge distances, the vast stretches of time,
are still there; our earth is still as infinitesimal as ever
in comparison with the whole universe; and we
human beings are still supposed to strut our tiny
hour on our tiny stage, and then to leave it as though
we had never been. That some few and exceptional

[1] *The Mysterious Universe*, Cambridge: University Press, 1930.

minds amongst us, the pure mathematicians, should be enabled to "think God's thoughts after Him" is, indeed, on such a view a sufficiently surprising fact; but it affords, in itself, little reason for assigning to man a privileged position in the scheme of things.

The line of thought just indicated will need to be much more thoroughgoing and radical if it is to succeed in restoring the conception of man as occupying, in a certain sense, the central position in nature from which physical science would seem to have dislodged him. Above all, it will need to be recognized that there is something inherently perverse in an attempt to crush the spirit of man by thrusting upon it the immensities of the material universe. A point of view must be gained from which the entire scheme of things, as represented by physical science, will be thrown into different, and, if may be, truer proportion. At any rate, it requires but little reflexion to realize that spiritual qualities are absolutely incommensurable with material magnitude; and that no accumulation of the one can in any way compensate for a diminution of the other. Moreover, it is obvious that if human lives and human institutions were to find a station anywhere in the universe, it was bound to be on some specific portion of it, and why this earth should not have been that portion it would be hard to say. To object that it is but a wandering speck of dust in the huge cosmic whole is clearly irrelevant. There is no rational ground for supposing that the highest products of creation must needs monopolize a prodigious area of the spatial realm rather than a relatively minute fraction of it. Even though one were inclined to accept the doctrine of Fechner, for which, indeed, he could cite eminent authority, that the stars and planets have souls, one would have no reason for assuming that their mental would be proportionate to their bodily equipment, or that the range of their intelligence would exceed that of human beings. There is, in short, no common term by means of which we can compare spatial or temporal extent with intellectual or moral qualities. Who, then, will presume to decide which is, in truth, the greater reality, the stellar depths or the mind of the astronomer that is able to contemplate them?

2. Let us, however, before going further, look at the matter from another point of view.

In 1863, eight years before the appearance of Darwin's *Descent of Man*, Huxley published a striking volume entitled *Man's Place in Nature*. In that work he brought forward a mass of scientific evidence to prove that "no absolute structural line of demarcation can be drawn between the animal world and ourselves" wider than that between the animals immediately below us in the scale. And it seemed to him to follow that "if any process of physical causation can be discovered by which the genera and families of ordinary animals have been produced, that process of causation is amply sufficient to account for the origin of man". In so arguing, Huxley had, of course, in view solely man's bodily structure, although he did express his belief that "the attempt to draw a psychical distinction is equally futile, and that even the highest faculties of feeling and of intellect begin to germinate in lower forms of life".

As a biological principle, the theory of evolution is established on a sufficiently firm foundation, although most biologists would now, I take it, be agreed that the influences which have been at work in determining that evolution are far from having been as yet reliably ascertained. But, so far as bodily structure and functions are concerned, the resemblance of man to the higher animals is notoriously close; and there is no avoiding the conclusion,—if, indeed, one wished to avoid it—that the human race was originally developed out of some mammalian stock, in a way more or less similar to that in which the mammals originally arose from lower forms. When, however, we come to consider man as a rational, self-conscious, personal being the case is otherwise. Mental development would seem to have culminated not in a mere difference of degree but in a decided and unmistakable difference of kind. In fact, Huxley himself declared: "No one is more strongly convinced than I am of the vastness of the gulf between civilized man and the brutes; or is more certain that whether *from* them or not, he is assuredly not *of* them. No one is less disposed to think lightly of the present dignity, or despairingly of the future hopes, of the only consciously intelligent denizen of this world." In short, to say of the human mind that its coming into being was prepared for by the existence of mental lives of a rudimentary and primitive type settles in no way its place in the scheme of things as a secondary or accidental product.

The vastness of the gulf to which Huxley was here alluding may perhaps be rendered manifest in the following manner. The animals most nearly akin in bodily structure to man—those belonging, namely, to the tribe of the so-called 'anthropoids'—have, *ex hypothesi*, existed on this planet for a considerably longer period than the human species. Accordingly, if length of time is of consequence in the evolutionary process, there has been greater opportunity for the development of their latent powers than there has been for those of man. Yet, so far as observation has extended, the anthropoids of the present day appear to resemble in practically every respect their ancestors of the remote past. They still choose forests as their places of abode, they subsist on the same kind of food, they adhere to their old habits, they evince no sign whatsoever of any approach to the ways of civilization. It is well-nigh superfluous to contrast their history, if history it can be called, with the history of mankind. Originally, doubtless, a denizen of forests or caves, man has long since ceased to be such. By degrees, through the course of untold centuries, he has succeeded in converting this earth into what may not inaptly be called a *human* home. Cultivated lands, towns and cities have effaced even the relics of his primordial habitations; he has trained and disciplined himself in the arts to such an extent that there is left hardly a region on the surface of the globe where the results of his ingenuity and creativeness are not in evidence. While adapting himself to his environment, he has been yet, in larger measure, gradually adapting the environment to himself. Again, if, as has been maintained, the earliest form of human society was the hunting-pack, or co-operation for the purposes of defence and aggressive attacks upon others, still from that stage of ruthlessness human beings have long since emerged; through their agency, states and social institutions of the most varied kind have come into being, and have provided the conditions without which the graces and refinements of a cultured life would not be so much as conceivable. Huxley himself observes that man alone "possesses the marvellous endowment of intelligible and rational speech, whereby, in the secular period of his existence, he has slowly accumulated and organized the experience which is almost wholly lost with the cessation of every individual life in other animals; so that now he stands raised upon it as on a mountain top, far above the level of his humble fellows, and transfigured from his grosser nature by reflecting, here and there, a ray from the infinite source of truth". In other words, largely through the instrumentality of language, and what language has rendered possible—literature, in all its wondrous variety,—we civilized men and women are conscious of being in the midst of a vast spiritual environment, more potent far in shaping us into the personalities we become than any merely natural environment could conceivably be. To use Kant's memorable dictum, reason or self-consciousness is that in virtue of which a man distinguishes himself from all else in his experience. As a rational being, man is, that is to say, not simply a part of nature; he has become an interpreter of nature; for him, nature not only *is* but has *meaning*, however far he may be from deciphering what that meaning in its fullness is. And, as a moral agent, in so far as he applies the ideal to the actual, in so far as he converts 'what is' into 'what ought to be', man is more than an interpreter of nature; he is creating that which, like a thing of beauty, is valuable on its own account.

All this was, of course, sufficiently apparent to a thinker so great as Huxley; and, thirty years after the publication of the volume to which I have been referring, he delivered a remarkable lecture in Oxford, in which he emphasized, in his own way, the very points on which I have just been insisting. In that lecture he tried to show that the process of evolution in nature furnishes no clue whatsoever to what *ought* to be the moral aim of man. "The practice of that which is ethically best—what we call goodness or virtue—involves", he here insisted, "a course of conduct which, in all respects, is opposed to that which leads to success in the cosmic struggle for existence. In place of ruthless self-assertion it demands self-restraint; in place of thrusting aside, or treading down, all competitors, it requires that the individual shall not merely respect, but shall help his fellows; its influence is directed, not so much to the survival of the fittest, as to the fitting of as many as possible to survive. It repudiates the gladiatorial theory of existence." Accordingly, he concluded that "the cosmic process has no sort of relation to moral ends"; that "the imitation of it is inconsistent with the first principles of ethics"; that man's progress depends "not in imitating the cosmic process but in combating it". "Fragile reed as he may be, man, as Pascal says, is a thinking reed; there lies within him a fund of energy, operating intelligently and so far akin to that which pervades the universe, that it is competent to

influence and modify the cosmic process. In virtue
of his intelligence, the dwarf bends the Titan to
his will."

This significant utterance called forth at the time
several vehement protests. The strict adherents to
the evolution theory could not understand what
seemed to them Huxley's strange recoil from accepting
the consequences to which, as they conceived, that
theory obviously led. "If the ethical man is not a
product of the cosmic process, what", it was asked,
"is he a product of?" And, from their point of view,
the objection was doubtless pertinent. It is needful,
however, to note here that the term 'cosmic process',
or rather let us say the term 'nature', is excessively
ambiguous. It may be used in an all-inclusive sense
to denote the universe in its entirety, as it was, for
example, in that series of Goethe's aphorisms, which
Huxley once translated into lucid and elegant English.[1]
In that sense certainly man, with his spiritual and
moral endowments, is comprised therein. But in the
Oxford lecture Huxley was thinking of 'nature' in
the narrower sense in which it was customarily employed by the writers he had in mind, as denoting,
namely, the sum of inter-related objects with which
natural science is concerned. It seemed obvious to
these writers that human beings, with all their
potentialities of thought and activity, were integral
parts of nature as thus understood. It was, they
contended, matter of common observation that human
beings develop and alter in character in accordance
with the circumstances in the midst of which they are

[1] As an Introduction to the first number of *Nature*, November 4, 1869.

placed. Their modes of perceiving and willing present themselves, it would have been urged, as so many events to be observed; and as, therefore, susceptible of scientific explanation. These evince themselves as just examples of the way in which the more simple become in course of time the more complex, and the conclusion was readily reached that the sort of questions with which we are confronted in dealing with man as a knowing and moral agent would be solved could we succeed in tracing the manner of development of the cognitive and conative processes, and of the formation of social customs, institutions, and so on. According to this view, human beings and all that is characteristic of them, are no other than *objects* about which we may gradually acquire information, objects presumably far more complex than any others in the sphere of scientific inquiry, but not involving features which render necessary a mode of investigation essentially different from that followed in regard to those facts the exact character of which it is admittedly the business of natural science to attempt to determine. However defective our knowledge of the part of nature distinguished as 'human' may be, it would be implied and taken for granted that the defect in question is only a defect in the number of details we have been able to ascertain, and that it would be remedied by the steady accumulation of further details, similar in kind to those we already possess, details such, for instance, as the anthropologist is continually supplying. It would be assumed that, although our knowledge of what essentially character-izes any one part of nature may be imperfect, yet the imperfection would be removed if we could discover the network of relations in which it stands to the other parts of nature, constituting with it the whole.

The bearing of the view under consideration may perhaps be more clearly brought out by aid of the following illustration, which I borrow from one of the popular writings of Fichte. "Suppose this grain of quick-sand to lie a few places further inland than it does;—then must the storm-wind that drove it from the sea have been stronger than it actually was; —then must the preceding state of the weather, by which this wind was occasioned and its degree of strength determined, have been different from what it actually was; and the previous state by which this particular weather was determined, and so on; and thus you have, without stay or limit, a wholly different temperature of the air from that which really existed, and a different constitution of the bodies which possess an influence over this temperature, and over which, on the other hand, it exercises such an influence. On the fruitfulness or unfruitfulness of countries, and through that, or even directly on the duration of human life, this temperature exercises a most decided influence. How can you know,—since it is not permitted us to penetrate the arcana of Nature, and it is therefore allowable to speak of possibilities,—how can you know that in such a state of weather as may have been necessary to carry this grain of sand a few paces further inland some one of your forefathers might not have perished from hunger, or cold, or heat, before begetting that son from whom you are descended; and that thus you might never have been at all, and all that you have ever done, and all that you ever hope to do in this world, must have been obstructed, in order that a grain of sand might lie in a slightly different place?"[1]

3. The view I have been depicting has been and still is widely current; and, on account of its affinity to the modes of thought which have been prevalent in the natural sciences, it has been proposed to designate it that of "scientific naturalism". There are, as we have seen, in recent times signs of a revolt against it on the part of scientific investigators themselves. But, so far, that revolt has been of a more or less half-hearted character; and has, I think, failed to bring to light the really vital consideration that is fatal to the view in question.

To some extent I have already indicated the line of consideration I have in mind. Let me, however, try now to exhibit it more in detail. I can perhaps best do so by reverting once more to the assumption on which the doctrine which we may, for convenience of reference, continue to name "scientific naturalism" proceeds. It proceeds, namely, on the assumption that 'nature' (including under that term human agents and all that characterizes them) is a sum-total of interrelated *objects*, which in virtue of these inter-relations are taken to compose or make up a whole.

In everyday life we are so familiar with the 'common-sense' distinction between the individual conscious subject and the objective world over against which the individual subject stands in a position it would seem of independence that we are apt to take what has perhaps a sufficiently harmless significance in ordinary practical intercourse as though it were a self-evident and unquestionable truth. Yet it needs but little reflexion to awaken doubts upon what has thus been taken for granted. For the very term 'object' is a relative term; it signifies *that which stands over against* a conscious subject in the relation of knowing. Now, in all matters of controversy, the ultimate appeal of 'scientific naturalism' is to the facts of experience. To the facts of experience, then, let us go. Does experience really warrant us in first of all distinguishing subject and object; and, then, having made that distinction, in forthwith treating the knowing subject as in like manner one of the objects of the known objective world? Does experience lend countenance to the notion that the entities we call 'objects' simply co-exist with the other entities called 'subjects', the latter being all the while themselves 'objects' with a specific character of their own? The answer can scarcely be doubtful. Even though it were possible to treat in some measure modes of knowing and willing on the part of a conscious subject as so many 'objects' about which scientific knowledge might be obtained, and as, therefore, falling into line with the objects constituting the external world, yet there would still remain infecting the position in question an inherent inconsistency which no ingenuity would be capable of removing. For the conscious subject has throughout been viewed as standing over against the world of external objects, as exercising in regard to it the quite peculiar functions of knowing and willing; and the conscious subject's status in that respect, as exercising, namely, these unique functions, has been altogether lost sight of in the attempt to look upon human experience as itself no other than a part of the objective world. In short, whenever we are tempted to treat *the knowledge of an object* as though it too were an *object* to be known we are violating in an unmistakable manner one of the clearest deliverances of experience, and nothing but confusion and error can result.

Certain consequences follow at once from what has just been said. On one of these I wish to lay stress. If by the term 'nature' be meant the sum-total of objects, then we shall be compelled to distinguish between 'nature' so understood, on the one hand, and the sum-total of reality, on the other. For the sum-total of reality, what we may call the intelligible world, must, as we can see from a cursory inspection of experience, contain both the objective, the known realm of external fact, and the subjective, that which knows. Mind, that is to say, is no less necessary to reality in its completeness than 'nature', in the sense indicated. Yet it would obviously be thoroughly misleading to represent the intelligible world as the arithmetical sum of natural objects *plus* conscious subjects. It is in no sense that. The interconnected system of reality involves a correlation between these of a far more intimate kind than that of mere juxtaposition. Conscious minds, in other words, stand to 'nature' in a relation absolutely other than that in which one object in nature stands to another object in nature.

In the notion of 'nature' as a sum-total of objects

there is involved the implication that the relations
subsisting between these objects, these parts of nature,
the links of connexion between them, are external
in character—such relations as, for example, hold in
the spatio-temporal sphere. For, if objects be conceived as units which in relation to one another
constitute a whole, they can be related and constitute
a whole only after the fashion of a mechanism,—and
by mechanism I mean in this context a system of
connected parts which has the peculiarity that the
action of any one part is determined by action from
without exercised on it by other parts. But this notion
of mechanical connexion evinces itself at once as
wholly inadequate when we try to interpret by its
means the sum-total of intelligible reality, including
therein conscious subjects, with their peculiar facilities
of knowing, feeling and willing. For the character
of a conscious subject is altogether incapable of being
understood by the help of any mechanical relations
assumed to subsist between it and objective facts.
Indeed, it is sufficient to point to the common language
of everyday life to show that so much is implicitly
recognized in ordinary practical conduct. We speak,
for instance, of influencing a mind by argument but
not of propelling it by physical energy; we speak of
a mind being attracted by persuasive reasoning but
not of its being attracted to the earth by the force of
gravity. In short, not only are the relations between
the phases or modes of the mental life altogether
different from the relations observed to hold between
constituents of the material world, but no one of those
phases can be described save by means of terms

quite other than those we employ in treating of the parts of an object. Thus, for example, in the act of apprehending or knowing a series of changing events there is evidently implied a unity of being of a quite unique kind. It is characteristic of every such act of knowing that the members of the series must be grasped not merely one by one as they come and go, but as a whole, in their totality. In so viewing them, the mind passes from earlier to later, from later to earlier, and contemplates the elements of the multiplicity together. Now, the unity of the cognitive subject which an act of this sort presupposes is utterly incomprehensible as being itself merely a series of events, such as that which it contemplates. We may speak of the cognitive act in question as being a mental event; but by the very qualification 'mental' we imply that it is an event in the life of a mind possessing a genuine unity. Otherwise, it would, at the most, be a series of awarenesses—I do not think it would be even that— but certainly not the awareness of a series.

One would have, indeed, no difficulty in bringing forward conclusive grounds for doubting the possibility of adhering consistently to the mechanical scheme of things even as a theory of nature conceived as merely a sum-total of objects. At the outset, those indispensable conditions of the being of nature, however mechanically conceived, continuous space and continuity of time, are certainly not 'objects'; and they are altogether inexplicable unless there be surreptitiously introduced into the notion of 'object' just that peculiar non-mechanical significance which no ingenuity can reconcile with a purely mechanical theory. Again, while the mechanical theory would exclude all reference to the qualitative,[1] yet it is obvious that the more we abstract from the positive features of things, the less adequate does our view become to express the whole fact which is before us in any perceived object. For instance, even were we ready to grant that material things only *appear* to be coloured or to be hot, and are not really so, still there would necessarily be *some* qualitative difference in the things themselves in consequence of which one thing appears to be red and another thing to be blue, or one thing appears to be hot and another cold. Probably of all the delusions to which human thinking is prone few are so insidious as the idea that qualitative distinctions can be discounted by pronouncing them to be 'appearances'.

In point of fact, the material world, as viewed by the physical scientist, is never actually conceived as consisting of mere mechanism. According to a rigidly mechanical scheme, what seem to us to be different kinds of matter are all, in truth, ultimately composed of homogeneous material; the apparently different kinds of matter are, that is to say, so many different configurations of particles which are alike in character, one material body differing from another only in the number, arrangement and movements of its ultimate constituents. Furthermore, on the theory in question the laws operative in nature are those which Newton

[1] It cannot, however, do so completely (cf. Professor Broad's remarks on 'pure Mechanism' in his book *Mind and its Place in Nature*, p. 44 *sqq.*). There is no getting under way at all without the assumption that the one stuff, out of which it is supposed every material object is made, possesses at least one intrinsic quality, e.g. inertial mass or electric charge.

formulated as the three laws of motion, or some substitutes for them. In other words, the behaviour of material objects is taken to be determined, solely and completely, by the pushes and pulls to which they are subjected. Now, however successful a thoroughly abstract conception of this sort may be in quite general fields of scientific inquiry, such as the dynamical theory of gases, no scientist really works with it when dealing with the concrete facts of the external world. The physicist is confronted with things and events which can by no device be accounted for by reference merely to changes in the configuration and motion of a so-called material system. The thermal, optical, electrical or magnetic properties of bodies— indeed, the facts of elasticity and of friction—lead to the recognition of *special* laws which are discoverable by empirical research and in no other way. Moreover, even in regard to the movement of atoms the theory we are discussing has become obsolete. In the series of researches started in 1913, Bohr at first pictured an atom as a mechanical structure, yet was at length compelled to acknowledge that it was constantly evading the limitations of the picture, and passing from one orbit to another in an entirely non-mechanical manner. Again, no less manifest is it that in the field of chemical science there is no making headway with the notion of mere mechanism. So far from assuming that material particles are, in the last resort, all of one type, the chemist is constrained to distinguish at least ninety different kinds of atoms, and refuses to commit himself to the assertion that the laws of their interaction are mechanically analysable. It would be futile to insist, *per contra*, that the differences between (say) an atom of oxygen and an atom of hydrogen may be no more than differences between the number and configuration of two different groups of similar elements, the laws of which are mechanically analysable. Not only would such a contention be the veriest surmise, without a vestige of evidence in its favour, but it would be for chemistry a perfectly useless surmise. In truth, according to the most recent chemical theory, while the electrons of all atoms may be supposed to be similar, their nuclei must be thought of as differing in quality, and this difference of quality as accounting for the varied chemical properties of different substances. Once more, when it comes to dealing with the characteristics of chemical compounds the breakdown of any merely mechanical explanation is strikingly conspicuous. For example, from a specific amount of the two gases, hydrogen and oxygen, combined in certain proportions, water is obtained. But by no stretch of imagination can we picture, as it were, with the mental eye the qualitative features of water—its fluidity, for instance,—gradually coming into being through the mere putting together of these two chemical elements.

If, then, we acknowledge with Lotze how absolutely widespread is the *extent* of mechanism, we must likewise recognize with him how perfectly subordinate is the *significance* of the function which mechanism has to fulfil in the structure of the world. And here it is relevant to emphasize a further consideration, upon which, in another connexion, I shall have occasion to dwell more in detail later. The natural sciences (physics, chemistry, biology, and the rest) proceed throughout on the assumption that there is meaning, rationality, in the structure and behaviour of things, which meaning or rationality may, in some measure, at any rate, be fathomed by human reason and reflexion. Scientific inquiry raises insistently the question "Why"; and is animated by the firm assurance that ultimately it must be possible to answer "Because". An assumption I have named it; and, in one sense, it is an assumption. But it is the outcome of no blind act of faith nor a simple concession to common-sense. On the contrary, it is a necessary postulate of all scientific procedure; and its justification lies just in the impossibility of conceiving nature to be knowable if it does not contain within itself the conditions requisite for becoming known. It implies, in other words, that nature—the object of scientific knowledge—is logically constructed, that its parts are intelligibly related, and that such relationship can be expressed in terms of thought. To this extent, therefore, natural science is bound to be anthropomorphic; it has no alternative other than to work with the notions and categories that constitute the equipment of the human intellect. Take, for instance, the relation of cause and effect, the recognition of which Mill declared to be "the main pillar of inductive science". That relation is, in truth, a special form of the much wider relation which in logic is indicated by the term ground and consequent, one form, that is to say, of the ultimate demand for intelligibility which the human mind carries with it to the interpretation of all that it is said to experience. And the

principle of the relation of ground and consequent
is no other than the fundamental principle under
which the active work of human thinking is conducted,
the principle, namely, of connecting all the data with
which it is concerned into one intelligible system.

4. Looked at from one point of view, the positivist
doctrine, as likewise the more recent modified version
of it which in America goes by the name of "Humanism", may be said to be the precise opposite of what
we have been calling "scientific naturalism".

The positivists have persistently striven to enforce
the lesson that man, however feeble in physical
strength, is yet in his very feebleness superior in
essence and in significance to the blind forces of
nature; for, as Pascal expressed it, he knows himself
and they do not. The positivists have been strenuous
in insisting that between spatial magnitude and
mental or spiritual greatness there is no common
term; that, however marvellous may be "the starry
heavens above", even more marvellous still is "the
moral law within". "The man who reviles Humanity
on the ground of its small place in the scale of the
Universe is", wrote Frederic Harrison, "the kind
of man who sneers at patriotism and sees nothing
great in England, on the ground that our island holds
so small a place in the map of the world. On the atlas
England is but a dot. Morally and spiritually, our
Fatherland is our glory, our cradle, and our grave."[1]
Furthermore, in addition to emphasizing the consideration that the history of the human intellect and
conscience cannot be cast into modes of expression

[1] *Creed of a Layman*, p. 76.

appropriate to material events and processes, positivist writers have never been weary of inculcating the truth that the development of personality is only possible in the midst of a community or commonwealth of intelligent beings. To isolate the individual from society, they have argued, would be to deprive him of all that which characterizes him even as an individual. From the very first, the social factor is instrumental in building up his individuality. He thinks and learns by means of a language which is the language of his nation; from his neighbours he imbibes his tastes and habits and opinions; through the help of institutions into which the social body has organized itself, he loves his fellows and worships his God.

That these contentions have become now almost truisms detracts in no way from the credit due to those who did much to make them "current coin". It is, however, with some of the more distinctive features of positivist doctrine that I am here concerned; and in their light it will be evident, I think, that the opposition of positivism to scientific naturalism is not of the pronounced character which, at first sight, it would appear to be.

As the name indicates, positivism is based upon a view of what can be positively known, and this is taken to be the realm of actually experienced or observed fact. In respect to the physical universe, we know and can know, so Auguste Comte maintained, only phenomena, the appearances which things present to our modes of cognitive apprehension; it is vain to endeavour to penetrate beyond phenomena or to grasp the nature of so-called ultimate reality. Yet this world of phenomena is, he urged, in no sense a scene of merely haphazard occurrences; in the vast stream of events we find invariably uniformity both in co-existence and in sequence. Each single event evinces itself, that is to say, as an instance of a general law. And it is the business of science to bring to light these laws or uniformities, not, indeed, in order to explain phenomena—for that they cannot do—but in order to determine their manner of occurrence and thus to describe them. In this way, by discerning, namely, the interconnexion of events, we are enabled to anticipate what will happen in the future, all important from the human point of view; the essential aim of scientific research is, in fact, to see in order to foresee (*voir pour prévoir*). Abandoning, then, any attempt to reach an 'objective synthesis', a view of reality *in ordine ad universum*, Comte's belief was that the most we can attain is a 'subjective synthesis', a view of things *in ordine ad hominem*, confined, that is, to human beings and the phenomena of which they are conscious, and obtained by the co-operative labours of the present and past generations of men. Yet, as the culmination of this 'subjective synthesis', he conceived himself entitled to assert the reality of the *grand Être*, Humanity, "the most vital of all living beings known to us". "All our thoughts, feelings and actions spontaneously flow", we are assured, "towards a common centre in Humanity, one supreme Being— a Being who is real, accessible and sympathetic, because it is of the same nature as its worshippers."[1]

[1] See final chapter of Comte's *General View of Positivism*.

The tenets of positivism have been so exhaustively discussed by leaders of various schools of thought[1] that I may confine attention here to points bearing directly upon the subject we are at present considering.

I note, then, in the first place, that so far as a theory of knowledge is concerned the positivist analysis proceeds on the basis of a naturalism or empiricism of the crudest kind. For the data of our knowledge of nature we are solely dependent, so it is contended, upon the impressions of the senses; and such knowledge as we have is derived by processes of reasoning from those data. Consequently, whatsoever we may be said to know is exposed to a two-fold source of doubt; doubt, on the one hand, as to the correctness of the reasoning process itself, and doubt, on the other hand, as to the trustworthiness of what the senses reveal. In other words, our so-called knowledge is throughout relative; relative in respect to its logical accuracy and relative as regards its answering to any objective reality. "For all that we know to the contrary", wrote Frederic Harrison, "man is the creator of the order and harmony of the universe, for he has imagined it. The objective order of the real world may be (probably is) something infinitely more subtle and highly organized than our conceptions. The image of it we frame may be as little like the truth, as rough an emblem of it, as the picture-writing of a savage. Or, again, the objective order of the universe may be something infinitely more simple, and our

[1] See especially T. H. Huxley, *Lay Sermons*; Edward Caird, *The Social Philosophy and Religion of Comte*; J. Martineau, *Types of Ethical Theory*, vol. i, and *Essays, Reviews and Addresses*, vol. i; and Lord Balfour, *Essays and Addresses*.

disparate conceptions may be due, not to real differences but to idiosyncrasies of mind. Or (what is most
improbable) there may be no sort of real order at all
outside the mind, and our notion of order may be a
dream, just as a musician standing beneath Niagara
might hear some symphony in the Babel of waters;
though the music would be in the musician, and not
in the roar of the cataract."[1] Clearly, by "the mind"
is here meant the individual mind; it is the individual
mind that is represented as receiving impressions,
which always remain "a system of mental pictures";
it is the individual mind that is said to create "the
synthesis of nature" by a process of inference from
sense-impressions. Now, waiving the many embarrassing questions that at once present themselves as to
the possibility of there being any process of 'reasoning'
or 'inferring' on the part of a mind thus limited for
its equipment to sense-impressions, I would invite
attention to the ease with which it is assumed that an
individual mind, although utterly incapable of determining whether there be or be not a world of objects
other than that which it itself constructs out of sense-
data, is yet in a position to attain complete certainty,
not only as to the existence of other individual minds
than its own, but as to the reality of one "great Being",
comprising within itself all finite intelligences. If an
individual mind can so far transcend itself as to be
cognizant of so stupendous a fact as this would be,
on what conceivable plea can it be alleged that it is
constitutionally debarred from getting at the truth
respecting such things as tables and chairs, and even

[1] F. Harrison: *The Philosophy of Common Sense*, pp. 32–3.

planets and suns? It is futile to argue in this context that Humanity is "akin" to us, that it is ever "in touch" with us, and so on. If that be so, the question is how we become aware of it, and whether such awareness would not require a power of intellect at least adequate for discerning the real characteristics of external things. All talk about a "universal consciousness" is, we are told, "mere verbiage".[1] Be it so; but in that case might not a follower of Hegel justly retort that all talk about a "universal Humanity" must be of like character?

In the second place, the positivists are, as might be anticipated, strenuous in insisting that what it is now customary to call 'values' are, in truth, human creations,—"man as the great centre makes everything real". What, for example, are the beauty, the harmony and the majesty which we discern in nature? "Nothing but what man sees in it and feels in it. It is beautiful to us; it has a relation to our lives and our nature. Absolutely, it may be a wilderness or a chaos. The poets, indeed, are the true authors of the beauty and order of nature; for they see it by the eye of genius. And they only see it."[2] This view of the meaning of aesthetic values is not, of course, confined to positivist writers, and I hope to say something about it in a later lecture.[3] Here, however, I would simply register the fact that it has not been the persuasion of 'the poets' themselves. Their inspiration would have evaporated like morning dew had they anyhow been

---

[1] F. Harrison: *The Philosophy of Common Sense*, p. 137.

[2] F. Harrison: *The Creed of a Layman*, pp. 201–2.

[3] *infra*, p. 228 *sqq*.

brought to believe that they had been but romancing and projecting "psychic additions" of their own into the external world.

"If Nature be a phantasm, as thou say'st,
    A splendid figment and prodigious dream,
To reach the real and true I'll make no haste,
    More than content with worlds that only seem."

And, indeed, those engaged in other realms of art than poetry have worked in the confidence that they were giving expression to that which had been revealed to them and not to mere pictures of their own inventing. But more relevant for our present purpose is it to refer to the account which positivist writers have to offer of moral values. As in the case of the beauty of nature, so in the case of moral ideals; the latter, it is contended, are products or manifestations of human mentality. They exhibit, so it is held, in their formation and growth, unmistakable features that have emanated from the interaction between individual minds in the social community; and it is from reflexion upon what has been already achieved by the thought and institutions of men that conceptions of a better state of things to be attained in the future spring into being. Now, while it may readily be admitted that many social and political ideals do originate in some such way as this, it is clear, I think, that the theory breaks down completely when the ideals in question are those which are supremely characteristic of the moral life. For one thing, history testifies in the most unequivocal manner that every considerable step forward in the morality of a people has been accomplished by some great personality, endowed with a fullness of insight and a richness of character far beyond the level of his fellows. They are "the children of the *status quo*"; he is "one born out of due season". They build the sepulchres of the prophets and garnish the tombs of the righteous whom their forefathers slew; he is pleading for a further extension of the ideals which the prophets and martyrs cherished, for what they would have striven for had they been his contemporaries and co-workers. What he sees and reveres is something over and beyond what they saw and revered; and no mere survey of the past could have given birth to that which in the past had never been so much as contemplated. "The world is ever claiming as its own those who have indeed been in it but not of it. The very essence of a true reformer consists in his being the corrector and not the exponent of the common feeling of his day. The breath of his life is inspired from above, not drawn from below."[1] Moreover, the *obligation* which the moral man recognizes he is under of being faithful to the ideal disclosed to him and of doing what in him lies to 'realize' it is left by positivist writers wholly without theoretical justification. Frequently they have urged that the consciousness of duty or obligation is a secondary and derivative factor in the development of morality. In support of this contention, they have pointed out that the relation involved in obligation is of a very general character, and is not confined to the moral sphere. We feel

[1] T. H. Green: *Works*, vol. iii, in the essay on "The Force of Circumstances", p. 10.

constrained or obliged to assent, for example, to the proposition that two and two make four, and to any proposition expressing what is manifestly a fact. True, but not to the purpose; the circumstance that obligatoriness connects itself with much that lies outside the definite domain of moral action tends not in the least to undermine its essential significance within that domain. Further, it is alleged that the genesis of the consciousness of moral obligation can be traced to influences which do not imply or involve it. Such consciousness is, we are assured, of the nature of a habit generated from social pressure. Familiarity with the regime of compulsion, and the device of inflicting pain to deter from particular sorts of conduct, is accordingly represented as the first germ of the feeling of obligation. Then what began as fear of incurring penalty gradually assumes the character of fear of giving pain to those who are respected and esteemed, until finally the reasons for imposing the restraint come to be appreciated, and fear is transformed into an inner monitor that seems to stand "upon an independent foundation". There is thus supposed to result an internal "ideal resemblance of public authority", "an imitation within ourselves of the government without us"; so that, though at first derived and imported, conscience takes on at length the aspect of being spontaneous and self-legislative. It is, it seems to me, a sufficient reason for rejecting all such modes of explanation that they altogether fail to account for that which beyond all else calls to be accounted for. Moral obligation is *not* compulsion; and, disguise or refine the latter how you will, you will never succeed in showing that it can be converted into that which is wholly devoid of compulsion. Duty enjoins but does not coerce; and, if the recognition of what is right does not awaken the consciousness of obligation, naught else in the world will avail so to do. Society may punish the evildoer; yet it will not thereby force him honestly to confess "I ought not to have done this". An error it undoubtedly was to contrast, as Kant was inclined to do, duty on the one hand with inclination and impulse on the other, as though these were necessarily opposed. On the contrary, the highest type of moral character may be said to be that in which the whole of the individual's dispositions have been brought into constant and habitual conformity with the requirements of duty. But, although in the concrete life of mind recognition of the imperative of duty is an element in a complex, the essential point is that the imperative itself is, at any rate, *sui generis*, an ultimate fact which cannot be resolved into simpler constituents. And were it not so, certainly one of the strongest and most cogent reasons for conceiving the status of man, as the positivist writers have done, to be unique and pre-eminent in the world of nature would be withdrawn.

In the third place, it is evident that the "great Being" was repeatedly envisaged by Comte as an actually existent entity, capable of receiving help and of reciprocating love. "Man as an individual cannot", he tells us, "be properly said to exist except in the exaggerated abstractions of modern metaphysicians. Existence in the true sense can be predicated only of Humanity."[1] What exactly the true sense of the term "existence", as here used, was supposed to be I make no attempt to conjecture. But, without trying to determine this, it may safely be asserted that, not only by "metaphysicians", but by ordinary common-sense persons, an individual man *would* be said to exist, indeed to be a typical example of an existent. And equally unquestionable is it that in that sense, whatever it be, Humanity would *not* be said to exist. In asserting that an individual man exists we imply, *inter alia*, that he is something that *has* certain characteristics, such, for example, as the capacities of thinking, willing and loving. On the other hand, in speaking of humanity, we do *not* imply that it is something which *has* characteristics; we use the term to express the characteristics themselves, conceived in abstraction from any individual who has them. Clearly, however, Comte was not employing the term "Humanity" in the way just indicated; and was not, it must be confessed, consistent in adhering to any one specific usage. Frequently, he spoke of Humanity as a "collective being", as an *esprit d'ensemble*, and then would appear to signify a totality, comprising all the members of the human race.[2] No less frequently, he obviously implies, if he does not explicitly affirm, that Humanity is no mere collection or totality of individuals but an organic unity with a life and consciousness of its own, and that its development is the

[1] *General View*, p. 246.

[2] So, too, Frederic Harrison writes: "As every flake of snow that falls on the crest of Mont Blanc passes on from glacier to rill and thence to river, till it falls a drop into the sea, so does every life and every act of every life contribute to the sum of Humanity."—*Creed of a Layman*, p. 76.

unfolding of that organic unity which remains identical with itself throughout all its changes.[1] Whichever of these alternatives be adopted the difficulties confronting the position are sufficiently patent. A totality of minds presupposes the existence of the individual minds composing the totality; and, although these think and feel and will individually, it is manifest that, over and above their thinking and feeling and willing, there can be no thinking and feeling and willing on the part of the whole as such. On the other hand, if Humanity be an organic unity, the one truly existent Mind, while individual human minds are mere abstractions, then, doubtless, this existent Mind may be said to think and feel and will, but there will be no thinking and feeling and willing on the part of individual minds. It will not be they that think and feel and will, but the organic unity that thinks and feels and wills in them.

Since the days of Richard Congreve and Frederic Harrison the teaching of Auguste Comte has found few adherents in this country. Even the American "humanists" of the present day would wish to dissociate themselves from it. "Humanism", we are assured, "is not Positivism. Positivism as a religion is an artificial system which substitutes the 'worship of Humanity' (past, present, and future) for the 'worship of God',—'the immortality of influence' for the 'immortality of the soul', etc. Humanism, on the other hand, holds that the 'Humanity' of Positivism is an abstraction having no counterpart in objective reality, and that most 'influence' far from being

[1] As, for instance, in the passage cited above, p. 75.

immortal is highly transitory. To humanism 'worship' means the reverential attitude towards all that is wonderful in persons and throughout all of life; a wistful, hopeful, expectant attitude of mind; not abject homage to either 'Humanity' or 'God'."[1] Nevertheless, other 'humanist' writers are to be discerned using language—excessively vague and rhetorical, it is true,—which would simply have no meaning had they not had in mind some such conception as that we have been considering. For instance, one of them, Professor C. H. Lyttle, of Meadville Theological School, writes: "It is evident that we are all children of Humanity, our eternal parent, whose fecundity seems undepleted, notwithstanding the innumerable generations of men already brought forth on the earth. All the spiritual values of life, all the moral excellence of mature personality, all the fine potentialities of frustrated lives are seminal in her streaming energies. All the virtues which constitute large and lovable character are implicit in that prior parental source from which the multitudes of the future will derive their origin."[2] And another, a well-known writer, speaks of 'humanity' as "the mother-matrix in which we are all equally conceived and bred and born".[3] In the light of statements such as these, the line of demarcation between the two positions would seem to be scarcely appreciable, and I have been unable to discover any new feature of importance in the more modern doctrine. Indeed, one meets with some

---

[1] *Humanist Sermons*, edited by Curtis W. Reese. Chicago: Open Court Co., 1927. Preface by editor, pp. vi–vii.

[2] *ibid.*, p. 33. [3] Frank C. Doan, *ibid.*, p. 229.

strange vagaries in the utterances of the American 'humanists', against which certainly the leaders of positivism would have vehemently protested. Take, for example, a confession such as the following. After singling out as a "characteristic of the new religion" its different attitude towards the matter of theology, one writer proceeds: "Will it" (i.e. the "new religion") "require a belief in God? I think not. Personally, I am inclined to be somewhat of a mystic. I find a quality in the universe that is akin to myself; the quality that manifests itself in order, in beauty, in creative activity, in love. And I like to call this God. However, it does not disturb me in the least that other men come to different conclusions and feel that the facts compel them to describe the world and all things in it entirely in terms of blind force and matter."[1] How either the self or God can be a "quality" and how a "quality" can manifest itself in creative activity, it would be futile to inquire.

The truth is that according to positivism (or 'humanism'), no less than according to scientific naturalism, man is "like a stranger in a foreign country, who seeks to arm himself with such fragments of knowledge about it as are necessary for his protection and his own private ends".[2] To attempt to deify Humanity and to worship it as God is, in short, no less perverse an undertaking than to seek to trace back all mental life to the blind working of material mechanism.[3] For quite obviously Humanity is not

[1] E. Burdette Backus, *Humanist Sermons*, p. 74.

[2] Edward Caird: *Social Philosophy and Religion of Comte*, p. 143.

[3] Indeed, if Humanity be conceived as the great *Ensemble* of individual persons, as a 'collective unity', we are landed in the end into the position

the self-contained and self-subsistent being which the language used by the positivists has so often implied. Even Comte himself had to admit that Humanity is not literally self-contained. Even he was compelled to acknowledge that human development takes place in a 'medium' or environment—an 'external fatality', he named it,—furnished by the natural world. But what he strenuously refused to recognize was that human development has been dependent not only upon a material but upon what we have called a spiritual environment. Yet, as I hope to show in some detail later, the reality of this spiritual environment is abundantly confirmed by any impartial survey of the relevant facts. Meanwhile, let me illustrate my meaning by referring again to the sphere of morality. It is not too much to say that moral progress of a decisive kind, whether of an individual or of society, has invariably found its inspiration in a divine 'discontent', a conception of a Best that is beyond the good manifested in any human life which has so far been lived. For every significant advance which has actually been attained towards even a 'relatively Better' we are indebted to those who were assured that in the realm of the spiritual there was an ideal of the Best, which they could, dimly and imperfectly, discern. Or, as Professor A. E. Taylor has impressively urged, the virtues which ennoble human life are all

of the purely naturalistic doctrine. For so conceived, Humanity, it would have to be allowed, must emerge into being at some particular stage of the world's history. Before there could be such a 'collective unity' there must needs be units to form it. And this implies on Comte's premisses that human life and intelligence must originally have sprung from non-human or non-spiritual conditions.

of them to be met with in their purest form only where human society is not made the *principal* end and the *supreme* object of loyalty. It is, he contends, one of the great lessons of history that mankind itself is most truly served by "those who feel the duty of serving it to be one they owe to something more august and worthy to be loved than humanity".[1]

> "The faith that life on earth is being shaped
> To glorious ends, that order, justice, love
> Mean man's completeness, mean effect as sure
> As roundness in the dew-drop—that great faith
> Is but the rushing and expanding stream
> Of thought, of feeling, fed by all the past."

[1] *The Faith of a Moralist*, vol. i, p. 349.

III

RELIGIOUS EXPERIENCE

1. The Duality in Unity of Experience. 2. The Nature of early or rudimentary Experiencing. 3. Religious Experience conceived as religious Feeling. Schleiermacher's conception of Religion. 4. Religious Experience regarded as immediate. 5. Mystical Experience.

WHEN religious minds have discarded the ecclesiastical doctrines of the final authority of the Church and of the Thirty-nine Articles, and no longer rest their faith on the infallibility of the Scriptures or on a miraculous revelation in the past, it is natural for them to turn to individual experience and to find in it the ultimate basis of religious trust. We experience the Divine directly and immediately, many of them would urge, we are conscious of actual personal intercourse with God. Belief in God, that is to say, grows out of an intuitive affirmation of the individual's own consciousness. And I shall try to show that when rightly understood these statements embody a profound truth. But 'religious experience' is a phrase which calls for a good deal of careful scrutiny. The best way of bringing out what I conceive it ought to signify will be, I think, to revert first of all to the conception of 'experience' generally, about which something was said in the first lecture.

1. At the outset, I would insist that if under the term 'experience' be included all we know and feel and do, all our emotions and ideals and ends, it is imperative to recognize what, as we saw, James Ward described

as the duality in the unity of such experience. On the one hand, there is that which is or may be experienced; and, on the other hand, there is the mental act or process of experiencing. When experience is said to be, as it frequently is said to be, a phase of conscious life, which an individual subject undergoes or passes through, the emphasis is being laid upon the latter of these aspects. When, however, F. H. Bradley contended that "sentient experience is reality, and what is not this is not real", he was meaning by 'experience', pre-eminently at least, that which is experienced. In fact, he admitted that he himself could "conceive of nothing else than the experienced".

Now, just because it is essential to recognize the two-fold reference (*a*) to that which is or may be experienced and (*b*) to a process of experiencing, it .is, I would submit, impossible to accept the dictum that "everything is experience". It is, indeed, by no means easy to determine what exactly Bradley wished to have understood by this proposition. Often he certainly seemed to imply that all the so-called 'things' of nature are psychical in character. "There is", he wrote in one place, "no being or fact outside of that which is commonly called psychical existence. Feeling, thought and volition (any groups under which we class psychical phenomena) are all the material of existence, and there is no other material, actual or even possible." What seems to be asserted by a statement such as this is that any object which we feel, or think, or in regard to which we will, itself consists of feeling or thought or will, or of some complex of these. And, by way of clenching the position, we are challenged to "find any piece of existence, anything that any one could possibly call a fact, or could in any sense assert to have being, and then judge if it does not consist in sentient experience".

It is, I take it, clear that any plausibility this argument may be supposed to possess arises solely from the ambiguity of the term 'experience'. If by that term be meant a mental process of experiencing, then there is no difficulty in responding to the challenge. For to allege that 'things' consist of sentient experience in this sense is merely to assert what, on the face of it, seems to be directly contrary to fact, without producing a shred of evidence in support of the contention. If, on the other hand, be meant by the term in question the whole complex situation, awareness of a fact or an existent, then doubtless we cannot produce that of which we are not, to some extent, aware; but nothing is thereby settled as to the nature of the said fact or existent. Whatever its nature, that would still be true. There is certainly no sense in which we can "continue to speak of it when all perception and feeling have been removed". But that would still be the case even though it be as different from perception and feeling as a material entity is usually taken to be.

Although he would be far from acquiescing in the dictum that "everything is experience" a natural scientist would probably argue in favour of a theory involving what has been aptly named a "bifurcation of nature". He would, that is to say, differentiate nature into two divisions, into the nature apprehended in awareness and the nature which is the cause of that awareness. "The nature which is in fact apprehended in awareness holds within it the greenness of the trees, the song of the birds, the warmth of the sun, the hardness of the chairs, the feel of the velvet. The nature which is the cause of awareness is the conjectured system of molecules and electrons which so affects the mind as to produce the awareness of apparent nature. The meeting point of these two natures is the mind, the causal nature being influent and the apparent nature effluent."[1]

It wants no small amount of care to disentangle what has virtually been implied in this 'bifurcation' theory. One of these implications is, however, evident. The individual mind has been regarded as functioning after the manner of a so-called 'thing' or object in the external world; it is supposed to be operated upon by mechanical means and to re-act mechanically. Now, although this is usually taken to be a fact beyond dispute, it is, in truth, no more than an assumption, and an assumption which is really destitute of any justification. That there is a process of sense-stimulation no one need be concerned to call in question. But sense-stimulation is a bodily process, and not, so far as can be discovered, in any respect a mental one. In the case, for example, of visual apprehension, what the physicist is wont to describe as 'light waves' undoubtedly impress upon or stimulate the eye; and, in consequence, delicate changes occur in the cones of the retina, the fibres of the optic nerve become thereby affected; and the influence, whatsoever be its character, is conveyed by the optic nerve fibres to the

[1] A. N. Whitehead, *The Concept of Nature*, p. 31.

cerebral centres in the cortex with which the optic nerve is connected. Then, either concomitantly with, or in consequence of, the cerebral change, there ensues, not a patch of colour, not the awareness of one, but a mental state or mental act, in and through which, *when it is directed upon a coloured object*, there comes to be awareness of that object. And, on careful scrutiny, the cognitive act in question evinces itself to be invariably a process not of constructing, not of clothing with qualities of its own, that which it comes to apprehend, but of discriminating the features of an object already there, of gradually discerning distinctions not at first noticed, and of tracing connexions not at first recognized.

In short, we are, I think driven to the conclusion that there are no sense-qualities, such as colours, or sounds, or temperatures, *in* the mind. What is *in* the mind, when it is engaged in perceiving an external object, is the act of being aware of sense-qualities, which sense-qualities are presented *to* the mind but are not present *in* it. In the light of this conclusion, we need radically to change our ordinary conceptions not only of matter but also of mind.

On the one hand, the physical world can no longer be contemplated as consisting merely of quantitative elements, of huge complexes of atoms and molecules, or in the last resort of protons and electrons. For clearly, colours, sounds, temperatures, and so on, must be stationed somewhere; and, if they are not stationed *in* the mind, they must have their *locus* elsewhere. And where else can that be than in the external environment? Nor can I find in the scientific theory of matter and its properties anything which in the least conflicts with this contention. If the currently accepted theory be destined some day to be firmly established, then the protons, electrons, positrons, etc., which the physicist conceives he has brought to light, are veritable constituents of a physical object. But, all the same, there would be no ground for supposing these to be its *sole* constituents. Why should not the minute particles, the motions of which occasion the act of perceiving a red body, be themselves red; or, if they are not, why should not the whole complex of which they are constituents be so characterized? What is there to prevent *both* the red colour *and* the vibratory movements of the particles being present in the physical object, and these being specifically related the one to the other, in such a way that the vibratory motions, although they are neither identical with nor the cause of the colour, are yet the cause of the stimulation of the sense-organ which occasions the mental act of perceiving the colour?

On the other hand, nothing can well be more gratuitous than the notion that the mind throws up, as it were, from the depths of its being a great variety of different sense-qualities; and then, subsequently, through conscious acts of perception, becomes aware of these sense-qualities, aware of them, however, not as in the mind but as belonging to external things. Psychologically considered, the mental life manifests itself as a stream of conscious process, the modes of which it is customary to speak of as modes of perceiving, imagining, thinking, feeling, willing, and so forth. How this stream of conscious process could at the same time generate so-called 'secondary qualities' would be no less mysterious and unaccountable than how vibrating particles of matter could give rise to them. Moreover, it is scarcely possible to exaggerate the anomalous position of the mind, so conceived, stationed somehow in a universe composed of merely quantitative elements. One of the astonishing enigmas with which the history of human reflexion confronts us is, it seems to me, that the materialist of former days could rest so easily satisfied with the thought of minds thus amazingly creative making their appearance in the midst of an environment constituted as he took it to be.

It is, in truth, a prejudice to imagine that anything would be gained, so far as accuracy of knowledge is concerned, by regarding the contents of what is perceptually experienced as intra-subjective in character. In and through the process of cognizing, which, it need not be said, is always liable to error, we can no more be certain of the attributes of what is in our minds, if one may for a moment employ so metaphorical an expression, than of those of what is other than our minds. Indeed, were the contents of perceived objects merely complexes of subjective elements, it would be, as Edward Caird once wrote to James Ward, "as much a problem *how* we get *into* ourselves as how we get *out* of ourselves",—I should say, a far greater problem. The fact is, spatial metaphors are, in this context, altogether inappropriate. Nothing can be 'in' the mind, in any intelligible sense, save that which is mental in character.

Let us inspect now somewhat more closely the process of experiencing. Looked at genetically the successive phases of experiencing exhibit, as we have seen, innumerable grades of complexity dependent on the particular stage of development reached by the mind in question. But if we take the process of experiencing at the level with which we ourselves are familiar, we note at once the broad distinctions fixed in our ordinary nomenclature as those between knowing, feeling and willing. There is, it is true, no definiteness in the ordinary use of these terms, and it is not easy to get agreement in respect to their essential meaning. Roughly it may be said that the term knowing or cognizing indicates an attitude of mind, the being aware of something, which, however closely connected in concrete fact with feeling and willing, is yet in nature distinguishable therefrom. And similarly feeling, our mode of being affected—pleased or otherwise—with respect to our surroundings, would seem to possess a certain characteristic feature of its own. Of willing, one can speak with less confidence, for willing is obviously an extremely complex state of mind, involving factors both of knowing and feeling. Whether among its constituents there is to be found a unique conative factor is one of the most disputed points in psychology, upon the discussion of which there is no occasion here to enter. What, however, it is important to emphasize is that these three components, although logically distinguishable, are never really separable in the concrete life of a mature mind. Each is but a single function in the complex process of experiencing, and never actually exists apart.

2. These distinctions are, then, recognizable in the process of experiencing as it takes place in ourselves; and they indicate undoubtedly three lines, so to speak, along which the mental life develops. Yet we should not be justified in inferring directly to corresponding distinctions in more rudimentary forms of mental life. Indeed, on quite general grounds one would hesitate in proceeding on an assumption of that kind. It is, I mean, extremely unlikely that in the course of the evolution of mind changes of an important character should not have intervened between the primitive types and the more developed. I have just noted that willing is obviously complex and derivative. Consider, however, the perhaps still more ambiguous term cognizing. "In the phenomena of Cognition, consciousness distinguishes an object known from the subject knowing." So wrote Sir William Hamilton; and in substance this view has been prevailingly adopted. But, in point of fact, the subject-object relationship is one of the most difficult adequately to delineate in the whole field of theoretical philosophy; and, on that account alone, it would seem to be inadvisable to rest content with its appearing, in some one of its various meanings, in a description of the rudimentary stages of conscious experience. We can scarcely imagine that in what may be conjectured to have been the first steps towards developed knowledge, the crude apprehension, namely, of qualitative differences between sense-qualities, the conscious subject would already have been capable of drawing even the faintest distinction between its own inner state and an independent order of real fact. While there would be crude appre-

hension of the features of things which are in truth external, there would be no recognition that they are so. On the contrary, the evidence available points irresistibly to the conclusion that the conception—for it is a conception—of an independent order of fact grows up gradually, and is gained by a series of inferences from the relations and behaviour of the contents themselves. And, similarly, it is not to be supposed that in the early stages of conscious experience there is contained the conception—for, again, it is a conception—of the self, existing independently of and, so to speak, beyond the phase of momentary experience. A mind might be a conscious subject and remain such to the ding of doom without ever being aware of the fact. The awareness of self is obviously the result of a complex and complicated process; and must, therefore, be regarded as secondary and derivative.

Since it became manifest that neither knowing nor willing, in any of the ordinary senses of these terms, can be ascribed to the rudimentary consciousness, many psychologists have been induced to think that the simplest type of mental life would consist in feeling. In the beginning, it has been contended, there is nothing beyond what is and is felt simply. It is, however, not unlikely that those who have taken this view have been misled, and that they have confused the indefiniteness attaching to the primitive apprehension of sense-qualities with the vagueness attaching to the awareness of feeling in our mature experience. In our mature experience feeling is emphatically the personal or the pre-eminently subjective factor. What I feel I do not regard as an attribute of an object;

I regard it as a mode or way in which I am affected.
"The peculiarity of feeling", wrote Sir William
Hamilton, "is that there is nothing but what is subjectively subjective; there is no object different from self."
As subjective in this sense feeling is certainly not a
mode of knowing; we do not cognize in and through
feeling. But, although all this is so far true, yet if we
do not assume the distinction between subject and
object to be a primitively recognized distinction, we
are precluded from taking this "subjectively subjective" character to be a primary mark of feeling.
On the contrary, we are driven to the conclusion that
originally the experience of feeling did not involve
a definite reference of the feeling to the self or subject.
Feeling, we must suppose, acquires its "subjectively
subjective" character because its positive features (particularly those denoted by the terms pleasurable and
displeasurable) connect it constantly with what comes to
be recognized as the subject, and as constantly exclude
it from what comes to be recognized as objective.

On the ground of considerations such as these it
appears to me an error to describe a rudimentary state
of experiencing as coming under any one of the
familiar rubrics,—knowing, feeling, or willing. These
terms express generalities which roughly and imperfectly indicate broad differences that become manifest
in the gradual development of the mental life. What
we should expect to find, what I think we are entitled
to postulate, so far as the rudimentary components of
mind are concerned, is that, while such components
would be wrongly designated by any one of these
general terms, they contain in themselves the roots

from which the three diverging stems take their rise. If there be one general designation which may be selected for the earlier stages of mental life, it would be, it seems to me, the term 'activity', meaning thereby, however, nothing of the nature of exerting force or putting forth energy. In other words, even the most rudimentary mental occurrences would appear to involve an act of apprehending,—crude, chaotic, though it may be; and every act of apprehending, even the crudest, implies, so far as I can see, the elementary functions of discriminating and comparing. I can find no means of realizing what a state of experiencing can be which does not involve these simple functions, functions which in their more developed form are fundamental in conceptual thinking.

In saying so much about the primitive modes of experiencing I may seem to have been digressing. Yet the considerations I have been pressing have an intimate bearing upon the questions with which we shall be concerned in discussing the nature of the experience specifically designated 'religious'. And there is one other point upon which I would lay stress before proceeding to the topic before us. I have urged that mental life does not start as self-conscious life, that it gradually attains to self-consciousness. What I would now emphasize is that the transition from consciousness to self-consciousness is by far the greatest, by far the most momentous, advance ever made in the history of mind; or, indeed, for a matter of that, in the whole course of organic evolution.[1]

---

[1] "Das Selbstbewnsstsein ist das eigentliche Wunder in der Psychologie." —Windelband, *Einleitung in die Philosophie*, p. 337.

The consciousness of self on the part of an individual subject has had, as we have seen, its history. In its simplest and crudest form it would present features little removed from those of what has been named (misleadingly, I think) mere "sentience"; there would be but few characteristics whereby the individual would be aware of himself as marked off from what is not himself. And the whole history of the human mental life may be looked upon as the gradual process through which there has grown up, on the one hand, increasingly definite apprehension of the inner life as peculiar to the conscious subject; and, on the other hand, of a world of objects as distinct therefrom. The development of these two aspects of the act of apprehending must be conceived as strictly correlative; the one would be inexplicable apart from the other. "Man in becoming spirit, i.e. self-conscious and reflective, acquires being for himself over against the world and sets to work mediately making himself by his conduct in it."[1]

3. There has been a marked tendency amongst theological writers of recent times to discountenance the influence of the intellect or the knowing factor in the formation of the religious consciousness. "The whole apparatus of reason in religion", we are told, "has retreated in importance, in favour of a more substantial basis—which we have agreed to call feeling."[2] "Religious experience", declared the Danish philosopher Höffding, "is essentially religious feeling." While a well-known American psychologist

[1] James Ward, *Psychological Principles*, p. 463.
[2] W. E. Hocking, *The Meaning of God in Human Experience*, pp. 37-38.

writes: "What the future of religion is to be no one can tell. Of this, however, I think we may be sure: religious belief will stand or fall with what I have called the religion of feeling."

I propose to look at this view as it was set forth, more exhaustively perhaps than elsewhere, in the works of Schleiermacher. Although he contrived to labour in the midst of the reformed churches of Germany, Schleiermacher was virtually attributing to religion quite another function and quite another significance than that which had been assigned to it by orthodox tradition.

As a philosophic thinker he sought to surmount the antithesis which seemed to him to lie at the basis of all reflexion upon the world and man,—the anti-thesis between the real and the ideal. Though in the actual world the antithesis would appear to be suffici-ently prominent, it cannot, he maintained, be con-ceived as absolute; we are compelled to postulate a transcendental ground of being in which the real and the ideal, existence and thought, are united. The individual soul itself involves the union of the anti-thetic factors, for self-consciousness, that which is basal in human nature, supplies an expression of the fact. Seeing, then, that we have in ourselves an instance of the identity of thought and existence, we are forced, so Schleiermacher maintained, to conceive that under-lying the antithesis manifested in the world there is an absolute identity of these factors. Above all, in religious experience, we have assurance of the ultimate oneness behind the endless multiplicity of contrasts; the "religious consciousness of the unity of the intellectual

and physical world in God" is our best guarantee of
the truth of the cardinal principles of philosophy.
Neither member of the antithesis must be thought of
as producing the other; they are both equally con-
stituent elements of the world; but in God they are
one. Consequently, God and the world are distinct.
Nevertheless, they are correlative, and neither can
be conceived apart from the other. Without God the
world would be "chaos"; without the world God would
be an empty "phantasm". But, though transcendent,
God is immanent in the world; and, so far as our
self-consciousness is the unity of the real and the
ideal, God is immanent in us.

It was, I take it, this notion of the divine immanence
in the soul of man that lay at the root of Schleiermacher's interpretation of religious experience. The
true nature of religion, he averred, is neither the idea
of one single being outside the world and behind it
nor any other, but just "the immediate consciousness
of the Deity as He is found in ourselves and in the
world". The self, the person, is an individualization
of the supreme Mind; and the being of God is
involved in the very fact of our personality. I shall
have to consider the notion of immanence in the next
lecture. Meanwhile, I note that difficulties at once
arise when we proceed to inquire as to the precise
nature of this assumed "immediate consciousness" of
Deity. At successive periods of his life Schleiermacher
used different terms by which to indicate its character.
In the early edition of the *Reden* he called it a feeling
or intuition of the universe, awareness of the Infinite
and the Eternal within the finite and the temporal.

Although he refused to regard it as a mode of knowing, he yet spoke of it as implying both contemplation and feeling. But, as I have striven to make clear, these are in truth very different functions, and if we seek to determine how there can be contemplation apart from any cognitive activity we find ourselves baffled. Not only so. When in such religious contemplation we are said to have in view the 'universe' in its totality, our perplexity is enhanced. For what lies before us in any moment of contemplation can be no more than a limited group of objects, whereas the universe, the whole of being, is only to be grasped, if indeed it can be grasped at all, by means of conceptual thought or rational reflexion. It was, presumably, in consequence of his coming to realize the incompatibility of the two positions he had thus been inculcating that Schleiermacher in his later writings (in the *Glaubenslehre*, for instance,) virtually abandoned the notion of contemplation, and defined religion as "a feeling of absolute dependence" on the Divine. Religious feeling lies, then, in his view, beyond the sphere of knowledge; it is purely subjective or immediate in character; and in it the divine spirit loses any vestige of foreignness or estrangement, and becomes blended, so to speak, with the consciousness to which it is revealed. Not when He is set before us as a Being to be thought of or reasoned about have we the deepest assurance of God. On the contrary, it is when His presence penetrates the soul and takes possession of it, when we feel that the certainty of His existence is identified with the certainty of our own. Doctrinal propositions, such as that all things are caused or created by God, belong to the rationalized system of ideas by means of which men seek to draw out the implications of the feeling of absolute dependence, but stand in no essential relation to it.

Now, the term "feeling" is, as I have said, woefully ambiguous, and it would be unfair to assume that Schleiermacher was using it in any one specific psychological sense. Yet he certainly did definitely contrast it with cognition and will; he certainly did suppose that feeling could exist in and for itself, and entirely fill the sphere of consciousness. In other words, there are, in his view, phases of consciousness in which no elements of knowing or willing are involved. But, so conceived, it remains true that feeling never is in our mental life present alone or in isolation. Feelings do not float about promiscuously in the stream of mental process like fish in a river; they are experienced always in intimate conjunction with some mode of exercise of either the intellectual or volitional functions. On this account, while it is possible theoretically to conceive of a mental life purely cognitive in nature, it is not possible, so far as I can see, theoretically to conceive of a mental life consisting entirely of feeling, if by the term 'feeling' be meant a consciousness devoid of the facility of cognizing. There are doubtless cases in which feeling seems to obliterate everything else and to extinguish both consciousness of self (as when we say of an individual that he is 'beside himself') and of the objective world. These are, however, emotional states; and emotional states are unquestionably mental states of extreme complexity in which processes of thinking and willing, confused in content though they may be, are certainly implicated.

In speaking of a 'feeling of *dependence*' Schleiermacher had, in fact, given his case away. Mere feeling could not proclaim its own nature, could not thus distinguish itself from the various feelings we have with respect to the objects around us. The very circumstance that a religious man is conscious of his dependence upon the divine Being is a sufficient indication, in itself, that the dependence has not been, so to speak, thrust upon him, that it has been discerned by him through a cognitive act of his own. In fine, it is senseless to talk of *religious* feeling unless we mean thereby feeling that is engendered by religious ideas, ideas of what are taken to be spiritual verities. The phrase 'absolute dependence' is nonsense if it does not imply a reality to some extent known on which to depend.

4. There can be little doubt that Schleiermacher was frequently, though not, I think, always, employing the term 'feeling' in the way it is now customary to speak of 'immediate' or 'intuitive' experience. But here, again, we are met with the difficulty that this phrase is beset with ambiguity.

We are said, for instance, to immediately experience our own mental states or processes. Every phase of the mental life is *at once* a mode of apprehending, or being aware of, something, *and* a mode of what, in the absence of any better mode of expression, may be called 'being for self'. Consciousness of an object is never merely consciousness of an object; it is always at the same time an *Erlebnis*, a state or condition (*Zuständ-*

lichkeit) of 'living through' that phase of consciousness. But the character or nature of a mental process is in no wise disclosed by the 'immediate experience' which we are said (misleadingly) to have 'of' it. If we ask *what* it is that is thus being immediately experienced, we get no answer from immediate experience itself. By means of another act of consciousness we may reflect upon that mental state and distinguish it from others; but to 'live through' (*erleben*) a mental process and to know that we are 'living through' it are two very different things. And the difference may perhaps not inappropriately be described as the difference between feeling and cognizing. Now, when Schleiermacher spoke of "self-consciousness in its immediacy" it was probably 'immediate experience' in the sense just indicated of which he was thinking. Once more, however, it has to be insisted that by no stretch of imagination can 'immediate experience', as thus understood, contain within itself a "consciousness of unity with the Eternal".

Again, an act of perceiving an object is sometimes described as an act of 'direct' or 'immediate' apprehension. It is now unreservedly recognized by psychologists that perception as it takes place in ourselves is an extremely complex process. And yet, on account of the obvious instantaneousness and clearness of outline with which objects often appear, it is natural for those who are not psychologists to regard vision, for example, as resembling the mere receptiveness of a photographer's plate rather than as the result of mental activity. But take such an instance as the visual apprehension of a tree. The slightest reflexion will enable us to realize that much more is therein involved than a merely passive acceptation of a given object. We recognize that the object is a tree and name it so to ourselves, a recognition which obviously presupposes prior experience in large quantity. And even if we assumed without further inquiry that the form, the visual shape, of the object in question is directly apprehended, we should still have to admit that *this* shape or *this* figure is determined by us as of a particular kind. We call the thing in question a tree and not merely a visual object. That is to say, we distinguish *this* particular object from other particular objects and compare it with them. Clearly, therefore, there are involved in such an act of sense-perception three factors at least, (*a*) the actual presence of the object, (*b*) the revival or recall of what has come before the conscious subject in past experience, and (*c*) that activity of discriminating and comparing to which we ordinarily give the name of thinking. And it would be easy to show that a large number of what are called thoughts or concepts—such as those of reality, externality, permanence, and so on—are implicated in the perception in question. I am not, however, now attempting to offer a psychological analysis of the process. I am concerned simply to point that, despite the fact that a large number of conceptual factors are involved in our perception of particular objects, the apprehension of the object in such cases appears to the conscious subject apprehending to be direct, immediate, intuitive. The knowing subject seems, as it were, to *stand over against* the object (the *Gegenstand*) and simply to know. And this very circumstance that the apprehension of objects with spatial and temporal relations of a complex and complicated kind thus appears to us to be direct and immediate is in itself sufficient to show that we cannot take 'immediateness' to indicate some peculiar and unique characteristic of some kinds of apprehension as contrasted with others.

The truth is that well-nigh everything which enters into human experience may, under certain circumstances, appear to the experiencing subject to be given in the form of immediacy. Such apprehension may seem to be simply direct and immediate apprehension of a content because at the time nothing of the nature of mediate inference is detected in it, although, as we have just seen, that is no guarantee that mediate inference is in fact absent. Taking, then, 'immediacy' in this sense, it is important to note that it may evince itself in two quite different ways. There is an immediacy that would seem to be above the level of rational mediation, but there is also an immediacy that is below it. And we shall see presently it is the cardinal defect of what is usually called mysticism that it ignores this vital difference.

Consider, first, the latter of these. When from our own standpoint we endeavour to retrace the steps along which the development of mind has proceeded it becomes obvious that what characterizes the earlier stages of mental life is partly the relatively small number of ways in which it is exercised. Pre-eminently, however, what characterizes the earlier stages is, as I have already indicated, the relative confusedness, the want of definiteness and precision, in the content apprehended. Let me illustrate what I mean by quoting a well-worn example of Hutcheson Stirling's, used by him, however, in a different context. "When one morning the day broke, and all unexpectedly before their eyes a ship stood, what it was was evident at a glance to Crusoe. But how was it with Friday? As younger and uncivilized, his eyes were presumably better than those of his master. That is, Friday saw the ship really the better of the two; and yet he could hardly be said to see it at all." What to Crusoe was a ship was to Friday only an "amorphous blur, a perplexing, confusing, frightening mass of details".[1] Now, in one of the senses in which the term is used Friday's apprehension of the object may be said to have been more 'immediate' or 'direct' than Crusoe's, in the sense, namely, that there were certainly fewer conceptual factors involved in it. Yet, quite evidently, so far from being any guarantee of truth, such 'immediacy' was precisely the opposite.

On the other hand, there is an 'immediacy' that would seem to be above the level of rational mediation. There occur particularly to men of genius moments when ideas or thoughts, revelations of some truths or beauties not previously recognized, seem not to have been reached by rational reflexion but to have 'come', to have 'dawned' or 'flashed' upon the mind, all at once, as being given, so to speak, and not acquired. The mathematician sees, as it were, at a glance the solution of an equation the attainment of which would occasion the novice a large amount of labour. Lucky ideas, Helmholtz wrote of his own experience, "often

---

[1] *Text-book to Kant*, p. 54.

steal into the line of thought without their importance being understood; then afterwards some accidental circumstance shows how and under what conditions they have originated; they are present otherwise without our knowledge whence they come. In other cases they occur suddenly, without exertion, like an inspiration".[1] Consider another instance. The reported testimony of Mozart is well known, how he was accustomed to take in a piece of his own artistic work at one glance, like a beautiful picture, and hear it not consecutively, as it had to be expressed, but as it were altogether, as a whole. So, in like manner Wordsworth, in numerous passages, has left on record how visions of nature's splendour would steal unawares into his soul. And these experiences of the scientific discoverer, of the artist and the poet, no one would wish to gainsay. It is true doubtless that they cannot be gained by mere effort, yet it is no less true that without effort they cannot be gained at all. Ideas may illumine suddenly the minds of men of genius, but they have been prepared for by strenuous intellectual labour; they sum up in themselves, so to speak, in concentrated form the results of long and toilsome critical analysis and reflective reconstruction. They do not drop from the skies; they come to minds of wide range and profound depth, minds that are saturated with thoughts making for the new ideas and pointing the way towards them. And, even then, their claim to be experiences of what is true is entitled to recognition only in so far as they can stand the test of critical scrutiny and rational interpretation. Otherwise, they

[1] *Popular Scientific Lectures,* ii, pp. 283–4.

may be legitimately regarded as open to suspicion and distrust.

And as there have been Newtons and Darwins, Mozarts and Wordsworths, in whom the inbred capacity for science or art seems to need but a touch to spring into full vigour, and through whom lesser men obtain new conceptions of the world of nature and new ideas of beauty; so there have been men and women of religious genius to whom we owe thoughts of God and glimpses of spiritual things, which ordinary minds would not have attained, though, happily for them, they can appreciate the value of what has thus been made known, and count themselves well blessed in trying to realize its wealth of meaning and to guide their lives thereby.

5. In his recent work on morality and religion[1] Henri Bergson tries to show that there are two radically different types of religion as there are two radically different types of morality. In the field of morality there is, on the one hand, what he calls 'closed morality', the morality that is based on instinct, and which evinces itself in habits, customs, laws and institutions that hem men in and keep them confined within a narrow circle of rights and duties. On the other hand, there is what he calls 'open morality', the morality that owes its being to the men of moral genius, who foresee, as it were, intuitively a new social atmosphere, an environment in which life would be more worth living, a society such that, if they once tried it, men would refuse to revert to the old state of things. The former type of morality is ani-

[1] *Les deux Sources de la Morale et de la Religion.*

mated by fear, the latter by love. Correspondingly, in the field of religion, there is, so Bergson maintains, on the one hand, that type of religion which he calls 'static', "a defensive reaction of nature against what in the exercise of intelligence would be depressing for the individual and dissolvent for society". Religions of this type owe their origin to dread and misgiving; they are characterized by rites and ceremonies, which soothe and give a sense of security to "the frightened child of humanity". On the other hand, there is the type of religion he names 'dynamic', which comes into being through means of revelations vouchsafed to great souls who possess the facility of making the effort of concentration on the basis of intuition, and who become filled with the emotion awakened by what they find there revealed. He identifies this 'dynamic religion' with mysticism, but insists upon distinguishing between 'complete' and 'incomplete' mysticism. As contrasted with the latter, the aim of genuine mysticism is "the establishment of a contact, consequently of a partial coincidence, with the creative effort of which life is the manifestation". If it is not God Himself, such effort is of God. The genuine mystic is to be conceived as an individual who is capable of transcending the limitations imposed on the human species by its material character, and who thus, under the influence of a great emotion of love, seeks to continue and extend the divine activity.

I am not, of course, now intending to enter upon a discussion of Bergson's Philosophy as a whole. I want simply to dwell for a while on his view of mysticism and of mystic experience.

The terms 'mystic' and 'mystical' have been used in a variety of ways, and Bergson is in accord with not a few modern writers in taking religious experience in its most vivid, intense and living form to be identical in nature with the mystic's experience of Deity when it reaches completeness. Nevertheless, I venture to submit that to bring under one heading the fervid spiritual assurance of minds such as Maurice, Jowett or Martineau, the passionate conviction of poets such as Dante and Wordsworth in the presence of natural beauty, and the beatific visions of such diverse personalities as Plotinus, St. Teresa and St. Catherine of Siena, is bound to lead to confusion and error. William James, who certainly handled the matter sympathetically, specified two marks which when they characterize an experience entitle it to be called mystical. The first is its ineffability, the experient asserts of it that it defies expression. Its quality must, therefore, be directly experienced; it cannot be imparted to others. Mystical states are more like states of feeling than like states of intellect. The second mark is that such states seem to those who have them to be states of insight, of illumination, into depths of truth beyond the reach of the discursive reason.[1] And Bergson himself is emphatic in insisting upon the supra-intellectual character of true mystical experience; such experience, he urges, transcends the intellect, and is of the nature of ultra-intellectual

---

[1] *Varieties of Religious Experience*, p. 380 *sqq*. James adds two other qualities less sharply marked which are usually found: the transiency of such states, and the passivity of the mind in having them. "The mystic feels as if his own will were in abeyance, and indeed sometimes as if he were grasped and held by a superior power."

intuition. But it is surely impossible to claim for mysticism, so understood, the unanimous testimony of all saintly souls. Admittedly, very many of the greatest religious minds regard the mystic's experiences as due in large part to overstrained 'enthusiasm' or visionary piety, and urge that the mystic ignores or neglects some fundamental elements which are present in rich and effective religious consciousness. And to me it seems that there is a wide divergence between those who rest religious faith upon grounds of knowledge, in the widest sense of that term, and those who maintain the possibility of direct intercourse with the absolute Being through the avenue of a kind of abnormal transfusion or identification, in which the individual becomes "partaker of the divine nature".

Bergson allows that those who reach the stage of what he calls 'complete mysticism' generally, at any rate, pass previously through the stages of what he calls 'incomplete mysticism'. He allows also that frequently what would otherwise be only abnormal (and all mystical states are, on his view, abnormal) may be accompanied by what is distinctly morbid, so that the condition of the individual in question is a form of disease, a manifestation of hysteria. But he insists that there is no reason for narrowing the word 'mysticism' to cover the latter type alone. This may readily be granted, and I do not wish to refer to cases that would be admitted to be pathological in character.

It has certainly been a prevalent belief among mystics that, in order to attain union with the Divine, everything belonging to the life of sense, everything belonging to our earthly environment, must be rigorously excluded. From the days of Plotinus and the pseudo-Dionysius, through the early and Middle Ages, down to our own times, the *via negativa*, the pathway of negation, has been set forth as the one way of approach to the mystical consciousness. No finite signs or symbols, no one of the categories of human thought, are, it is contended, applicable to the infinite Being. Neither existence nor non-existence, declared Dionysius, can be predicated of God. God is not this or that; He is beyond all the similitudes of our limited understanding. Meister Eckhart's favourite expressions when speaking of Deity are: "the nameless Nothing"; "the Naked Godhead"; "the immovable Rest"; "the Still Wilderness, where no one is at home". And his pupil Tauler wrote: "God is a pure Being, a waste of calm seclusion—as Isaiah says, He is a hidden God". "The quiet Desert of the Godhead, the Divine Darkness—this Abyss is our Salvation."

Thus, then, for the mystic, God is the absolute One, the ultimate Unity in which all differences are dissolved, even the difference of subject and object. The highest Reality is to be conceived as that which has least content; and pure being, the thinnest of all abstractions, is supposed to be something more real than is to be found in any specific mode of existence. But, most assuredly, pure being so regarded is at the widest possible remove from the living, personal Deity of the Christian faith. There is, in truth, no mystery whatsoever about the notion of 'pure being'. *Being* is simply the fundamental category of thought, which denotes everything and cannot, therefore, specially denote anything; or, in other words, connotes nothing. That which every entity is cannot be a property by which one entity is distinguishable from others. God, whatever else He is, must certainly be, but so must a triangle, a pebble in the street, a planet or a sun. In short, there can be no 'being' which is simply and purely 'being'; it is what God is over and above mere 'being' that is of primary significance for the religious consciousness. And, as a matter of fact, while insisting that the nature of Deity can never be apprehended by, or expressed in terms familiar to, a finite mind, the mystics invariably do ascribe qualities, such as oneness, wisdom, goodness and love to Him whom they worship, qualities with which the finite mind is well familiar and which are not inscrutable.

Again, it has been repeatedly maintained by mystics of all ages that if we are ever to enter into union with the Infinite, we must divest ourselves of all that belongs to our individuality—sense, thought, desire, the relation of subject and object—we must attain to a condition in which the individual mind is a blank so far as definite content is concerned. "During the short time the union lasts", averred St. Teresa, "the soul is as it were deprived of every feeling; and, even if she would, she could not think of any single thing. Thus she needs no artifice, in order to arrest the use of her understanding; she remains so stricken with inactivity that she neither knows what she loves, nor what she wills. In short, she is utterly dead to the things of the world, and lives solely in God." Continually to be met with in mystical literature are such phrases as "the nothingness" of the finite soul when in the condition of ecstasy, its annulment and absorption in the Godhead, its being merged and lost in the Infinite Spirit. Only when the individual soul becomes as nothing can God enter in and no difference between His life and the individual's remain outstanding. "This overcoming of all the usual barriers between the individual and the Absolute", wrote William James, "is the great mystic accomplishment. In mystic states we both become one with the Absolute and we become aware of our oneness."[1] But we are confronted here with what on the face of it wears the aspect of a palpable inconsistency. If in mystic states the individual becomes one with the Absolute, if in such states, as we are told in the *Theologia Germanica*, "there neither is nor can remain any I, Me, Mine, Thou, Thine, and the like", then how can *we* "be said to become aware of our oneness"? It requires a conscious self to be aware of 'oneness'; and if 'we' have reached a stage in which we are no longer conscious selves, such awareness, on our part, is *eo ipso* precluded. In that case, the awareness would be God's awareness, not ours; we cannot, at the same time, both be and not be. As Dr. Tennant has tersely put it, "the mystic cannot have it both ways". If he knows the Absolute as an Other, he cannot be this Other; if he has become this Other, *he* cannot know it, because *he* has ceased to be.[2]

The essential point on which, however, in this context to lay stress is that not only in attempting to describe but in actually undergoing his experiences,

---

[1] *op. cit.*, p. 419.   [2] *Philosophical Theology*, i, p. 320.

the mystic is constrained to interpret them. For he is, after all, a thinking being; and, do what he will, he cannot exclude the intellect from participating in any of his mental functions. Even in soliloquizing with himself he is construing his experiences intellectually. For instance, in his states of ecstasy he is assured that he is directly confronted with the ultimate Reality, that he is grasped by a higher power, that he has an immediate intuition of God. But that which he accepts on the ground of what he takes to be immediate intuition is clearly an interpretation. His interpretation may or may not be a true one; with that I am not at present concerned. Whether true or false this interpretation implies that, prior to the experience in question, the mystic has acquired his religious beliefs precisely as his non-mystical neighbour acquires his, namely, through instruction and tradition, through habitual ways of thinking, and through rational reflexion. In other words, he brings his theological convictions to the mystical experience; he does not derive them from it. The seeming 'immediacy' of the experience need imply no more than that, at the moment, he is unaware of the fact that his mind is saturated with ideas previously entertained, ideas of previous suppositions, and their inferred consequents. When, for example, some of the mystics declare that in the stage of what they call 'contemplation' they have been able to 'see' how God can be three Persons, or in what wise the Virgin Mary had been assumed into heaven, nothing can be more obvious than that they 'see' what they have been by training and teaching predisposed to see. Had they been nurtured in the faith of Buddhism or of Taoism their mystic visions would unquestionably have been entirely different.

Now, when men and women of undoubted integrity and saintliness tell us that they have attained the beatific vision, that they have seen God face to face, they can, of course, be implicitly trusted so far as their own state of convincedness is concerned. But there is all the difference in the world between this *subjective* certitude and *objective* certainty. In the early weeks of the war with Germany hundreds of persons were firmly persuaded that a huge number of Russian troops had arrived in this country and were being sent over to France; but, as a matter of fact, these persons were under a complete delusion, due to their misinterpreting what was actually taking place. If, then, the mystic not only informs us of his own unshakable certitude but goes on to claim that his *interpretation* of what he has experienced is indubitably valid and objectively certain, we are entitled, without forthwith rejecting his statement, to pursue in regard to it the method of judicial sifting and critical scrutiny. We are entitled to consider whether his interpretation is consistent with the established facts of physical science and psychology. For instance, when we are told that in a condition of trance the mystic is conscious of being grasped by a higher power, of being 'possessed' by an agency other than his own, so that his faculty of attention is no longer under his voluntary control, we at once begin to reflect upon the way in which one soul, one spiritual being, can act on or influence another. In the relation of mind to mind, is the exercise of force or energy psychologically possible? Can we really conceive of an efflux of energy from another mind operating on our minds, in the presence of which our minds are as passive as the wind-swept waves to the force of the storm? Or is not a transaction of this kind inherently meaningless? There are, as we shall see later, strong reasons for thinking so. "To propel a mind by external force", Principal Caird once declared, "is a thing as unintelligible and impossible as to move a stone by argument or melt a metal by affection or love." And he went on to argue that it would not be aught but simply unthinkable and absurd to conceive of God as, by any mysterious application of power, propelling a soul into goodness, or injecting convictions into a thinking mind.[1]

I am far from wishing to suggest that the experiences of mystics are all on the same level, or are all of them of the nature of hallucinations. I desire simply to insist that if these experiences are to be impartially and philosophically judged we cannot rest content in accepting the mystic's own valuation of them. Because a mystic's experience has been for him the experience of "One, a divine Dark, and ineffable", it by no means follows that God Himself is merely "One, a divine Dark, and ineffable"—and so a Being removed from the region of concrete reality. Many a mystic has, doubtless, committed himself to an inference of that sort, but it is both possible and necessary unreservedly to reject it. Even Bergson acknowledges that mystical experience, left to itself, cannot provide the philosopher

---

[1] *University Sermons*, pp. 79–80.

with complete certainty. "It could only be absolutely convincing", he tells us, "if he had come by another way, such as a sensuous experience coupled with a rational inference, to the conclusion of the probable existence of a privileged experience through which man could get into touch with a transcendent principle." But why, I would ask, the need of a 'privileged experience'? Why should the normal rational intelligence of man be judged to be incapable of discerning spiritual verities? Certainly, the fuller the individual's life is of all that goes to constitute rich human experience the better equipped will it be for attaining knowledge of God. If the individual seeks to withdraw from the fullness of conscious experience, to abstract from sense, thought, desire and will, to suspend the natural functioning of all his mental faculties, then there is nothing further to be said, except, indeed, that on such a presupposition to speak of the possibility of a 'privileged experience' would seem to be a contradiction in terms. If, however, he brings to bear upon what is offered in experience his whole personal life in its concrete completeness,—intellect, reason, feeling, aspiration and love,—what ground is there for assuming that the divine reality will necessarily escape his ken? God must verily be a God that 'hideth' Himself, if human intelligence, in spite of all that it has accomplished in the course of ages, seeks in vain to know Him who is "the Father of lights, with whom there is no variableness, neither shadow that is cast by turning".

IV

RELIGIOUS EXPERIENCE—*continued*

1. The Distrust in so-called 'Intellectualism'. 2. The Feeling or Emotion of Reverence as characteristic of Religious Experience. 3. The Conception of the 'Numinous'. 4. The Notion of Divine Immanence. 5. The true Nature of Religious Experience. 6. Faith and Knowledge.

THE accounts of religious experience which we were discussing in the last lecture have, it will have been observed, not a little in common. Whether the term 'feeling' or 'intuition' or 'mystical' be employed to designate what is taken to be the distinctive feature of such experience, the essential point on which emphasis is laid turns out to be that there is for man an avenue of approach to God other than that of thought or reflexion.

1. The central fact of religious experience is, it is contended, that men attain to an 'immediate' assurance of the Divine Spirit by means of a faculty which is different from the intellectual faculty. The intellect, we are assured, can neither reach nor comprehend the Divine. And it is being pressed upon us by persons of various theological persuasions that reason moves, and must necessarily move, within a sphere of abstractions. It operates, and, according to this view, can only operate, with notions or concepts, which are formed by a process of analysis, a process by means of which some general feature or characteristic is artificially severed from the concrete whole to which it belongs, and is then dwelt upon for itself alone.

In this manner, so it is alleged, we lose touch with the rich and variegated reality lying before us, and content ourselves with singling out some few salient features of it.

> "We love colours and not flowers:
> Their motion, not the swallows' wings,
> And waste more than half our hours
> Without the comradeship of things."

More especially, it is frequently maintained, does the dissecting process of thought evince itself as disastrous in the sphere of religious faith, for it murders religious experience in the very act of dissecting.

Newman, for instance, has left on record how he came to regard the free play of the intellect, which in his youth he had countenanced, as the inlet for 'an all-corroding and all-dissolving' scepticism. It precipitates us into imagining that "there is no positive truth in religion, but that one creed is as good as another", for all are irrational. Indeed, so far as the mere intellect is able to guide us, no warrant, he held, can be furnished for preferring the religious to the irreligious point of view. "It is", he wrote, "a great question whether atheism is not as philosophically consistent with the phenomena of the physical world, taken by themselves, as the doctrine of a creative and governing Power." And in that wonderful poem, *The Dream of Gerontius*, he made the angel say to the passing soul, "it is the very energy of thought that keeps thee from thy God".

So, too, many great minds, at a wide remove in other respects from Newman, have bidden us observe how reason, relying on its own strength, sinks back, baffled and impotent, into doubt and misgiving, when confronted with the supreme concerns of man's moral and spiritual nature. Not through its means do we reach conviction of the existence of God.

> "I found Him not in world or sun,
>   Or eagle's wing, or insect's eye;
>   Nor thro' the questions men may try,
> The petty cobwebs we have spun."

It was through another avenue Tennyson averred that he had himself attained the attitude of certainty.

> "If e'er when faith had fall'n asleep,
>   I heard a voice 'believe no more',
>   And heard an ever-breaking shore
> That tumbled in the Godless deep;
>
> A warmth within the breast would melt
>   The freezing reason's colder part,
>   And like a man in wrath the heart
> Stood up and answer'd 'I have felt'."

What value are we to attach to admonitions such as these? If one looks back upon the time when Tennyson was writing,[1] if one ponders, indeed, on much that has happened since, one is constrained to acknowledge a certain measure of justification for the prevalent distrust of what is disparagingly christened 'intellectualism'. The *Aufklärung* of the last half or more of the nineteenth century undoubtedly accom-

---

[1] *In Memoriam* was first published in 1850.

plished much. The untenability, from the point of view of natural science, of the Biblical accounts of the origin of the universe, of the creation and fall of man, and so forth, was demonstrated with logical cogency. The whole conception of the miraculous, on the basis of which the orthodoxy of that time reposed, gave way in face of the overwhelming evidence that was being accumulated of the reign of law in the natural world. But the standpoint from which much of this clearing of the ground was effected was that of a rationalism which, if I may express it so, was not thoroughgoing, a rationalism which displayed no confidence in its own strength. Underlying the destructive work of its adherents, much of it eminently needed and called for, there was a consciousness of embarrassing limitations. A sceptical mistrust of the very principle they were wielding to such purpose as an instrument of negative criticism lay at the root of their procedure, and doomed it to helplessness. Human reason, which had proved itself to be equal to large undertakings when it was a matter of dispersing the crude fancies of the early world, they looked upon as incompetent when it came to be a question of evincing its own constructive power. Though reliable enough so long as it confined itself to the realm of the senses and of historical fact, human thought was deemed to be altogether unfitted to venture into regions of supersensuous realities. A radical defect of a constitutional kind precluded it from making any advance beyond the region of finite things and events. The part of wisdom lay, therefore, in candidly recognizing the limits of rational inquiry, and in relinquishing the mysterious 'Beyond', the Unknowable, to form a sort of playground for the emotions and the imagination to disport themselves at will.

It is even reported of Henry Sidgwick, who certainly never thus doubted the capacity of reason, that at the close of a long life of truth-seeking he was conscious of being under the shadow of a dismal cloud. In earlier years he had thrown himself with enthusiasm into that effort after religious liberty which had characterized the last half of the nineteenth century. But the result, he confessed, was not that which he desired or expected. "Freedom is won", he said, "and what does Freedom bring us to? It brings us face to face with atheistic science; the faith in God and Immortality, which we have been struggling to clear from super-stition, suddenly seems to be in the air; and, in seeking for a firm basis for the fight, we find ourselves in the midst of 'the fight with death'." I believe it has been a persuasion of this kind which has led numbers of earnest minds to acquiesce in the view that the intellect cannot aid us in matters of spiritual import, and to appeal to some faculty assumed to override it, vari-ously described as feeling, or intuition, or immediate experience.

All the same, I am convinced that it is a grave error thus to separate feeling and knowing, for such a separation, could it ever come about, would mean the extinction of both. And I want now to try to bring to the surface the error I take to be involved in the position I have been delineating.

In the first place, it does not follow that, because it

operates with abstract or general notions, reason is thereby disqualified for the function of apprehending concrete living realities. Without general notions, no knowledge, in the ordinary sense of the term, would be possible at all; refuse to use abstract notions, and you must remain, as Aristotle put it long ago, for ever dumb. But, while the knowing mind inevitably employs general notions, it may none the less attain, and largely through their means, to a knowledge of particular individual facts. Just as the word 'blue' is used to signify blue, although the word itself is not blue, so a notion or concept, although itself abstract, may be used in determining the nature of something that is extremely concrete. In the second place, reason is by no manner of means merely a capacity of forming and using abstract ideas; it is just as essential to recognize the unification and synthesis involved in the process of thinking or reasoning as to recognize the analysis which is perhaps its more obviously apparent feature. Reason is not only the facility of distinguishing and discriminating; it is the facility likewise of apprehending the real world widely and steadily and connectedly. Even in ordinary speech we call a person unreasonable whose outlook is narrow, who is conscious of one thing only at a time, and who is consequently the prey of his own caprice, whilst we describe a person as reasonable whose outlook is comprehensive, who is capable of looking at more than one side of a question and of grasping a number of details as parts of a whole. Thus it is that every great scientific generalization carries with it a more accurate and definite individualizing of the particulars in which it finds exemplification. Were, for example, the story true that it was a falling apple which first suggested to Newton the thought of the universal law of gravitation, then this falling apple must instantly for him have become transformed into a much more pronounced and distinctive individual existent than any falling apples had ever been for him before. By discerning in it an identity of character with all other moving bodies, he was, at the same time, determining with greater clearness and precision its specific nature and significance. Abstraction is undoubtedly one feature, and a very important feature, of the activity of thought, but its importance consists largely in this, that it renders possible modes of insight and discernment that would be unattainable without it.

Intellectual activity may, it is true, degenerate into a cold and merely logical process of ratiocination, that seeks to pass all things in heaven and earth through the sieve of its narrow formulae of elimination or excision; but to suffer this logic-chopping faculty, as Carlyle called it, to usurp the name of reason is simply to trifle with ordinary linguistic usage. Discursive thought is, of course, legitimate enough within its own field, Carlyle's sarcasm notwithstanding. Yet the field is a limited field, and thought is very far from being merely discursive or formal in character. Since the days of Kant and Jacobi, the distinction between *Verstand* and *Vernunft* has been a commonplace in German philosophy,[1] and since the days of

---

[1] The distinction really goes back to the time of Plato, who expressly differentiated διάνοια and νοῦς.

Coleridge the former has been translated into English by the term 'understanding' and the latter by the term 'reason'. Understanding was not, indeed, regarded by these writers as a merely formal or discursive mode of thought, but it was conceived as having for its sphere of exercise the world of sense-objects. As a matter of fact, however, the ripe human intelligence is never thus confined. Understanding and reason are not, that is to say, two distinct faculties; they are stages in the life of one self-conscious activity. The processes of knowing on the part of a scientific man are the same in kind and operate in the same manner as those of the religious mind; they call for the same watchful scrutiny, and when they satisfy that scrutiny they deserve the same trust.

In short, the mind of an intelligent being cannot be split up into separate and air-tight compartments; there is within it no feeling that is not more or less rationalized feeling, no volition that is not more or less rationalized volition; nor is there, on the other hand, any thought that is not suffused with feeling, and which does not lead to volition. The mind of man is essentially a unity in which these various factors necessarily imply each other. They are, that is to say, correlative ways in which the one central unity expresses itself. But if we ask what that central unity is which permeates the many-sided aspects of our mental life—its several activities of perceiving, imagining, believing and willing,—there can be but one answer: it is the facility of knowing or thinking, the facility, in other words, of self-consciousness. Knowing or thinking is not, that is to say, one of many faculties;

it is that which forms the basis of, that which characterizes and co-ordinates, all our mental activities. As
I have previously urged, it is only as knowing or
rational beings that we have a place at all in the
realm of existence, and participate in that which is
other than ourselves. And that in which we participate
is not merely a physical environment; for the human
soul there is a spiritual environment which means
more and counts for more than the things of the
natural environment which we can see and touch. It
is by interpreting this spiritual environment, at first
dimly, imperfectly and incoherently, that we gradually
become religious beings.

As a matter of fact, it is not *mere* feeling or *mere*
emotion that is really meant when it is claimed that
feeling or emotion is the ultimate root of religious
experience. The persuasion of the heart, that refuses
to yield to the questionings of the discursive understanding, is not mere feeling or emotion, but rather
feeling which is based upon knowledge, emotion
which has at its back the complex experience of a
lifetime. When Tennyson, clinging to his religious
assurance, asserted 'I have felt', he was really opposing
to doubt, not mere feeling as such, but his entire
personality, gradually built up by thousands of
judgments and practical decisions. As A. C. Bradley
has shown,[1] it will not do to take the stanza I have
referred to as signifying that for the poet the sole
ground of belief in God and in immortality is that
the emotions cannot be satisfied without it. For
such an interpretation would evidently not apply to

[1] *Commentary on Tennyson's In Memoriam*, p. 61 *sqq.*

numerous other passages.[1] I do not suppose for a moment that either Tennyson or Browning were actually intending to affirm that we can feel what we do not in any sense know, or that the 'heart' can testify to that of which the intellect is absolutely ignorant.

2. Religious experience, especially in its mature form, involves, then, all the factors which go to constitute human personality. It rests upon insight, and it develops as such insight becomes keener and more comprehensive. It is thus emphatically based on knowledge. It contains likewise the element of feeling, for, although there is no such thing as feeling apart from knowing, feeling or emotion is an essential ingredient in the complex experience. And, since religious impulses operate as a potent means of inducing men to reach after moral ideals, religious experience leads to the concrete realization in conduct of what the moral imperative enjoins; it involves, that is to say, a fully fashioned will.

Hitherto, in dealing with the second of these components, I have spoken generally of feeling in the singular. But we can distinguish various modes of feeling. Inasmuch as they are always incorporated with cognitive states, feelings can be differentiated, held, sustained, and I think also revived. For instance, we may distinguish the feelings that arise in conjunction with sense-perception, those that arise in conjunction

---

[1] As, for instance, when he asks (*In Mem.*, lvi) shall man

> "Who loved, who suffer'd countless ills,
>   Who battled for the True, the Just,
>   Be blown about the desert dust,
> Or seal'd within the iron hills?"

with the exercise of constructive imagination, the aesthetic feelings, and so on.

Kant, I believe, was the first moralist to do justice to the peculiar nature of the feelings that may be specifically called moral feelings. The feelings that attach to the conception of duty as such, to the representation of the moral law, could, he maintained, be only appropriately described as feelings of reverence (*Achtung*) or of respect (*Ehrfurcht*), the former having a more personal, the latter a more impersonal character. These feelings differ, he urged, markedly from the feelings which occur in connexion with a constraint exercised over conduct. They arise only when there is present to consciousness as a fact for the individual subject the relation between his individual conduct as the means for 'realizing' the moral end and the requirements of that end itself. They can in no way be regarded as more or less pleasurable or painful phases of feeling in general.

Similarly, we should expect to find a group of feelings which may be called religious feelings,—feelings, namely, which connect themselves with the conception which we form of God and of our relation to Him. And here I should like to refer to a striking treatment of this subject by the distinguished Oxford philosopher, Cook Wilson, in an address he gave in Christ Church in 1879.[1] The feeling of reverence, he insisted, presupposes the conception of a spiritual being, but a spiritual being transcending everything human. If, following Kant, we speak of reverence for the moral law, it is because we think of the moral law as a

[1] *Statement and Inference*, vol. ii, p. 835 *sqq.*

manifestation of the nature of the divine Spirit. No such feeling is possible for a mere formula. Something spiritual which we are unable adequately to describe seems to be present to us; and, without our will, to fill us with a unique emotion. "Just as the person who has a real experience of gratitude *must* believe that there is another actual person to whom he is so related that he is grateful to him, so the actual feeling of solemn reverence is only possible because we actually *do* believe in God. So, in such feelings, in the actual experience of reverence and solemnity we are believing (not fancying, not imagining); we *are* believing in God, for it is impossible to have them at all actually except through that belief".

In thus fixing upon reverence as the distinctively religious feeling, Cook Wilson was, it seems to me, giving expression to an important psychological fact.[1] It is not, indeed, greatness and mystery alone that evoke the feeling of reverence, but these only in union with the assurance of goodness and love. Again, we may readily admit that the feeling of reverence, in the true sense, involves that the individual experiencing it is firmly persuaded that his conception of the divine Being is a conception of an actually existent Reality. Cook Wilson appears, however, to have thought that it involved more than this, that it guaranteed, namely, the validity of that conception. But I can only reiterate what I have already urged that subjective certitude

[1] Kant had, however, already asserted that reverence is due to persons only. And in a posthumous work of his, the *Opus Postumum* (first published in 1920), we read: "There is a God, for there is a Categorical Imperative of Duty", obviously implying that the latter is dependent upon the divine Being.

and objective certainty are not the same things; a person may be absolutely convinced of the reality of what he conceives has been revealed to him, but the irresistibility of his private conviction does not in itself suffice to establish its truth. Whilst, then, recognizing to the full the significance and worth of the feeling of reverence, I cannot agree that either it or the experience in which it arises is in itself demonstrative proof of the existence of God.

3. The signal service which Professor Rudolf Otto, in his well-known work *Das Heilige*, has rendered to the philosophy of religion consists, it has been said, in his having shown that "as far back as we can trace the beginning of religion, the 'holy', even if it is no more than an oddly shaped stone, does not simply mean the strange or the formidable; it means, at the lowest, the 'uncanny', and the 'uncanny' is precisely that which does not simply belong to 'this' everyday world, but directly impresses us as manifesting in some special way the presence of 'the other' world".[1] Otto recognizes as being essential to religion in its mature form that God should be thought of by means of such concepts as Spirit, Purpose, Goodness, Self-hood. But he insists these concepts fail to do justice to the unique character of religious experience. We speak of the Deity as 'holy'; but 'holiness' is, in fact, a complex attribute. It includes moral conceptions, such as the conception 'completely good'; it includes, however, in addition a non-rational element, an element which eludes apprehension through conceptual

[1] A. E. Taylor in *Essays Catholic and Critical*, by Members of the Anglican Communion, edited by E. G. Selwyn, 1926, p. 75.

terms, yet which is the fundamental factor in religious experience. To this non-rational element, as he takes it to be, Otto gives the name of the 'numinous'; and he is concerned to show its uniqueness in religion throughout, from its crudest to its most exalted forms. Viewed subjectively, it is a state of mind perfectly *sui generis* and irreducible to any other. It is not merely a feeling of dependence. Rather is it a 'creature-feeling', the emotion of a creature overwhelmed by its own nothingness before an over-powering might of some kind. Furthermore, it is the awareness of a mystery inexpressible and incalculable. And, accompanying this awareness, there is the unique feeling of awefulness, beginning in the mind of primitive man as the feeling of 'something uncanny', 'eerie', or 'weird', and surviving in the feeling of exaltedness and sublimity characteristic of the developed religious consciousness. Viewed objectively, the *mysterium* possesses the qualities of might, power, of energy or urgency, of awful majesty. It is the 'wholly other', that which is quite beyond the sphere of the usual, the intelligible, and the familiar. Yet, all the same, it acquires another aspect, in which it shows itself as something uniquely attractive and fascinating. The 'numinous' thus becomes that which is sought after and desired and yearned for; it is "experienced in its essential, positive, and specific character, as something that bestows upon man a beatitude beyond compare, but one whose real nature he can neither proclaim in speech nor conceive in thought".

Whereas, when he discerned in reverence the specifically religious feeling, Cook Wilson was confining attention to religion in its developed form, Otto is trying to indicate unique modes of feeling that enter into religious experience in all stages of its history. But that he has not been successful in differentiating religious feelings from others seems to me plain. The feeling of being overwhelmed by a power of some kind may be occasioned by the eruption of a volcano or by the presence of a beast of prey, facts certainly of 'this' everyday world. The awareness of mystery, again, is not confined to the religious consciousness. Well-nigh any environment, sufficiently great or strange, such as a lofty mountain or an unusual hurricane, may occasion it. The feeling of awefulness, once more, is not necessarily a religious feeling. It may be experienced by a person who is confronted with a railway accident or a colliery explosion. And I fail to see that anything is gained in the effort to determine the nature of religious experience by trying to connect the feeling of the 'uncanny' on the part of primitive minds in the presence of certain earthly objects with the feeling of reverence that pervades the soul of the Christian in contemplating the God he worships.

It is, however, the contention that in the case of the numinous object, over and above the natural thing itself which is visible and tangible there are directly apprehended qualities not belonging to this workaday world, indicative of an unseen presence, with which we are here mainly concerned. Professor Otto appears to think that the fact, as he takes it to be, of there being immediate awareness of these numinous features, in conjunction with their evoking numinous feelings or emotions, is in itself a guarantee of the existence of a transcendent or supernatural reality. In the numinous experience there are involved, he insists, beliefs and feelings qualitatively different from anything that 'natural' sense-perception is capable of occasioning. Yet he himself asserts of these beliefs and feelings that they are "peculiar interpretations and valuations, at first of perceptual data, and then—at a higher level—of posited objects and entities, which themselves no longer belong to the perceptual world, but are thought of as supplementing and transcending it".[1] But, if these primitive beliefs are 'interpretations' of perceptual data, obviously, however immediate or direct they may seem to be to the individual in question, they do not, in truth, possess *the* immediacy that is claimed for them. And, as 'interpretations', they are clearly liable to error and illusion; what is supposed to be other-worldly may, as a matter of fact, be very much of this world. Take, for instance, the 'numinous' features suggested to the primitive mind by an oddly shaped stone. Would any theist in a cultured community admit for a moment that the 'uncannyness' which the primitive mind discerns therein is a veritable revelation to that mind of the supernatural? Is there any ground for assuming that the appearance of 'uncannyness' is other than a natural delusion incited in a way which is psychologically explicable, or that it differs in any essential respect from the child's dread of being left alone in the dark?

I am unable, then, to look upon Otto's attempt sharply to distinguish what is essentially characteristic of religious experience from the rational and the moral

[1] *Das Heilige*, English Tr., p. 117.

as any more satisfactory than other attempts of a
similar kind have been. It is, I cannot refrain from
adding, a curious characteristic of his treatment that,
after having persisted in regarding the 'numinous'
as a specific experience *per se*, occurring originally
in independence of any rational and moral experience,
he is yet constrained to acknowledge that there is an
a priori connexion between these in the developed
consciousness. When, however, we inquire as to the
nature of this further *a priori* factor, or as to how it is
possible that two such disparate modes of experience
as he takes these to be can be connected *a priori*, we
get no enlightenment. Appealing to Kant, he speaks
in this context of a process of schematization. The
non-rational numinous fact is, he argues, schematized
by the rational and moral concepts, and there is thus
yielded the complex notion of the 'holy', now richly
charged and complete and in its full meaning. But the
resort to Kant's conception of schematism cannot but
be pronounced to be an extremely unfortunate resort.
Just as Kant's way of taking thought as purely the
source of universal categories, and sense-data as
merely particulars, and then looking for a middle term
by which to connect them, involved an abstraction
which, if he had consistently adhered to it, would
have rendered such a middle term impossible, so
Otto's way of taking the numinous as purely non-
rational and the rational as consisting merely of
concepts involves an abstraction which precludes him
even from so much as indicating any middle term by
which to bring them into union. Treat the numinous
as strictly non-rational, and it is simply incompre-

hensible how it could ever be clothed with the ideas of goodness, mercy and love.

4. The theories of religious experience which we have been considering—that it is based upon feeling, or upon immediate intuition, or upon mystic illumination, or upon a non-rational numinous faculty—all presuppose, if I mistake not, a conception of the immanence of the Divine in nature and in the mind of man which would, if consistently adhered to, undermine any attempt to sustain a genuinely theistic view. And I want now to make clear, if I can, why I think so.

That we are in the midst of an environment that is not merely natural but is also spiritual or supernatural in character we may lay down, I take it, as a plain fact of human experience in its higher forms. No intelligent person of the present day ever does, in truth, regard his environment as merely a vast assemblage of material elements, nor yet of these elements in conjunction with a multitude of other existents which we call mental lives. These constituents are certainly there; but no less certainly is much else there, entities, namely, which do not partake of the temporal character that material and mental existents exhibit. These timeless essences ($\iota\delta\acute{\epsilon}\alpha\iota$ or $\epsilon\acute{\iota}\delta\eta$), as Plato called them, and about which in another lecture I shall have more to say, may emanate from Mind, but they do not, at any rate, emanate from our minds. They are no creations of ours; we do not impose them upon our environment, we find them in that environment. The physical scientist, for example, is constantly striving to bring to light amidst the multitudinous variety of phenomena which it is his business to explore the laws or principles which these exemplify, and which are unaffected by the passage of months and years. The artist, again, is unweariedly seeking to embody some aspect of ideal beauty which, if he is true to his art, he never suspects to be a chance freak of his own, but takes to be a subsisting reality in the universe of being. So, too, the moralist is continually attempting to disclose the standard or norm of intrinsic worth, according to which conduct or character should be fashioned, and which if 'realized' in an individual personality would enable everything of value to be got out of life that life has in it to yield. These timeless verities belong, then, to our environment no less unquestionably than rivers and mountains. They are not, indeed, material existents; neither are they mental existents. But they have a mode of being of their own, which, while intimately related to the realm of existent fact, is not part of it. Moreover, they give to the natural environment a significance it would not otherwise possess; instead of consisting merely of brute facts, that environment thus becomes pregnant with meaning and symbolic reference. And the presence of these spiritual essences in the environment which we experience and know has repeatedly seemed to devout minds a conclusive proof of the immanence of God in the world and in the soul of man.

On the one hand, the order and intelligible plan, the grandeur and sublimity of earth and sea and sky —these reveal, it is claimed, to every discerning eye the existence of Him of whose ceaseless activity they are manifestations. "An active principle", Wordsworth declared, subsists—

> "In all things, in all natures, in the stars
> Of azure heaven, the unending clouds,
> In flower and tree, in every pebbly stone
> That paves the brooks; the stationary rocks,
> The moving waters and the invisible air,
>
> .   .   .   .   .
>
> from link to link
> It circulates, the soul of all the worlds."

And Wordsworth liked to picture the one infinite spiritual life as differentiating itself indefinitely into a myriad subordinate centres of life in nature, which could at any moment 'realize' the undivided life of the whole, but each of which also lived a distinct life of its own. It was God Himself that rejoiced in the sparkling brook, in the running stream, and in the sunlit hills; but the stars had their own tasks, the silent heavens their 'goings on', and every flower enjoyed the air it breathed.

It was a magnificent effort of imaginative insight; and far be it from me to suggest that underlying it there is not a profound truth. Yet it does seem to me that it is often taken to establish something very different from what it really does bear witness to, and that in consequence we are prone to suspect it, although in all likelihood we could not tell exactly why. Let me try to bring out what I mean in this way. God is a mind, the supreme Mind, a spiritual or self-conscious Being, the supreme spiritual Being—that is the cardinal affirmation of religion. Yes; but in our use of the terms 'spiritual', 'divine', and the like, there is a prevailing ambiguity; and it is an ambiguity against which in the present context it behoves us especially to be on our guard. We may designate that a divine or spiritual reality which we conceive to be the object of God's contemplation, of His approval, of His solicitude; or we may mean by divine or spiritual that which is a phase of God's actual life or being, as an act of thinking or willing is a phase of our own. Now, it is in the former sense and not in the latter that we speak, or ought to speak, of truth or beauty or ideal good as spiritual or divine; they are the features of the universe upon which God's mind would love to dwell; and in which He would, as Browning expressed it, constantly 'renew His ancient rapture'. But they do not constitute His mind, as an existence, any more than they constitute ours; they are not to be identified with His thinking, His feeling, His loving, any more than with our own; and His living soul or consciousness is not necessarily precisely there where they shine forth. Dependent upon Him they needs must be, if He be the sustainer of all that is; but to suppose that He, as living mind, is immanent in nature in the way they are is surely a grievous error, and an error that tends to bewilder rather than to aid the religious consciousness. Spiritual life, when thus conceived, loses for us its distinctive character; we represent it to ourselves as a sort of attenuated vapour filling every crevice of spatial extension, but as bereft of that inwardness, that individuality, of being which is the very essence of conscious existence.

On the other hand, when God as a real existing mind is said to be immanent in our minds, when it is maintained that God thinks in us and we in Him, the confusion is worse confounded. As existent, self-conscious beings, each of us is impervious to other existent, self-conscious beings, impervious in a way in which the impenetrability of matter is no adequate analogy. Mental states, as I have said, do not hover about promiscuously, waiting to be taken in by receptive minds; they are essentially states of one self, and, apart from that self, they have no mode of existence whatsoever. In and through knowledge and love, I can, it is true, transcend myself, and gain access to kindred souls; I can share in their life and interests, and feel for them an attachment of the deepest and purest kind. But this does not mean that their states of mind enter into or penetrate mine; it does not mean that our respective states of knowing and loving become fused into one and thus become identical. On the contrary, as an *existent* entity, each self resists invasion; it has no power of entering into another self or of admitting another self within its own. You and I may be apprehending the same natural fact, but my awareness of it cannot be the same as your awareness of it. As *existent* entities it is strictly true that—

> "Here, in the sea of life inisled,
>   With echoing straits between us thrown,
> Dotting the shoreless watery wild,
>   We mortal millions live alone."

So, too, is it in reference to our relationship to God, and His relationship to us. God may know a finite soul through and through, and feel towards it solicitude and love; a finite soul may know Him in whom it believes, and feel towards Him reverence and love. Yet, if God be an *existent* conscious subject, His consciousness must be in *Him*; must be *His* consciousness, and cannot be the consciousness of any other subject whatsoever. In other words, God's consciousness, as belonging to God, cannot be in me or in any other person; that would be possible only if my existence and God's existence were one and the same. It has, indeed, often been urged that we should be cautious in assigning to the divine Being a subjectivity similar to our own. And no doubt we should be. All the same, if we are to think of God as really existing, subjectivity, existence for self, analogous to our own self-existence, though immeasurably transcending it, is an essential factor in the conception.

5. It follows, therefore, that in religious experience we do not apprehend the mind of God in a way similar to the way in which, through introspection, we apprehend our own mind. But that is true also in respect to our knowledge of one another. There has been a considerable amount of discussion recently concerning the manner in which we become aware of other selves. The older view that the existence of a mind other than our own becomes known to us originally through inference by analogy from what each of us finds to be true in his own case in regard to bodily expressions and movements it is now generally agreed is untenable. And there has been a tendency of late to base such knowledge upon an assumed direct relation between two selves, in addition to the perception each has of

the other's bodily presence.[1] I am by no means convinced by the arguments advanced in support of this
theory, but I do not propose to enter here into a
detailed discussion of it. It will be sufficient to
emphasize two or three points that are relevant to
our present inquiry. In the first place, whatsoever be
the nature of the mutual *rapport* which is thus assumed
to subsist between persons, it certainly cannot be
maintained that through its means we are directly
apprehensive of the mental states or processes taking
place in another mind. If that were the case, the
science of psychology would be in a far more advanced stage of completeness than any of the natural
sciences! In the second place, whatsoever be the nature
of the knowledge we possess of other selves, it is clear
that such knowledge is never obtained in isolation,
but only through and in connexion with knowledge
of the bodily appearances and bodily activities of
those other persons. And, in the third place, I need
scarcely reiterate that we are not justified in taking
the terms 'direct' or 'immediate' to mean, any more
in this context than in others, that nothing of the
nature of interpretation or reflexion is involved.

In religious experience, it is, I venture to submit,
likewise impossible that we can be directly apprehending the actual states or phases of the supreme
Mind. However vivid and profound a man's religious
experience may be, he can be conscious of God only
through the medium of God's manifestations or working in the universe (including therein, of course, finite

[1] See, e.g., C. C. J. Webb's Lecture on "Our Knowledge of One Another,"
in the *Proceedings of the British Academy*, vol. xvi, 1930.

minds), and through the emotions thus awakened. Or, in more technical phraseology, just as I am convinced of my friend's existence through being aware of his essence, so I may be convinced of God's existence through being aware, however imperfectly and inadequately, of what I conceive to be God's essence. Again, I think it true to say that we can never experience the Divine in absolute isolation from everything else; we experience the Divine only through and in correlation with what is other than the Divine. In religious experience the devout soul is conscious of being in communion with the Divine Mind. That communion is acknowledged to be dependent on nature for its means, and to avail itself of the resources of nature. Nevertheless, while nature is admittedly material for expressing or revealing the presence of the divine life, it is never of itself taken by the experient to be the source of that life or the basis of it.

There is, then, so far as I can see, no insuperable difficulty in recognizing that God may commune with man in a manner analogous to the way in which one finite mind communes with another. Important differences of course there must be. For instance, since we experience other selves only through and in connexion with their bodies, other selves are supposed by us to be more or less confined in their operations to those situations in which their bodies are found. In the case of the supreme Mind, however, we do not suppose that there are any such restrictions. Well-nigh any situation may serve to reveal what we take to be divine, although there is no situation which invariably does so. The 'manifestation' or 'revelation' constitutes, as such, the objective side of the experience,—that which expresses or symbolizes the divine reality. On the other hand, the subjective means of experiencing or interpreting what is thus presented are more or less circumscribed and inadequate; and the consequence is that the 'manifested' or the 'revealed' assumes to a varying extent, for the individual, a pictorial or imaginary form. If, therefore, the language of religion be interpreted literally, it loses, in so far, its religious significance and hardens into crude dogma. But it need not be interpreted literally; it is possible for men and women of discernment to pass from the symbol to the symbolized. Accordingly, there have been and are those who look upon the evolution of religious experience in history as implying both a continuous process of self-disclosure on the part of God and a gradual process of 'realizing' the significance of that disclosure on the part of man. Beginning with the primitive religions of nature, where the spiritual breaks up, as it were, into an innumerable plurality of weaker and stronger, poorer and richer, spiritual beings, they would trace the advance to that phase where the spiritual is conceived as having its centre in selfhood as such, where one of its primary modes of expression is to be found in the moral consciousness, and where art serves as a means of external embodiment. And finally, in the highest stage so far reached, in Christianity, they would discern religious experience of a richer and more comprehensive import still. The Divine is then experienced not merely as 'the Lord of Hosts', not merely as (the Power not ourselves working for righteousness), but as the intimate companion of the pure in heart, as the inspirer of love, because love is an essential attribute of God's Being. Further than that, Goethe indeed declared, religious experience can never attain.

That religious experience of the kind just depicted has been a pervading influence in the lives of earth's largest and most balanced souls, the spring at once of their aspiration and their strength, is not to be gainsaid. Such an experience must, for example, have been Plato's when he heard from the lips of those who had been present in the prison of the way in which Socrates had spent his last hours on earth, of how he had spoken to them quietly and dispassionately of his anticipations of what was in store for the soul; and then, in the calm assurance that no 'evil can eventually befall a good man, had gone cheerfully forward to explore the future. Such an experience, again, was Dante's when he, meeting Beatrice with her two companions, seemed, as he expressed it, to touch "the very limits of beatitude". Beatrice passed away on the threshold of her womanhood, but the glorified memory of her gracious gentleness and virtue became for him the protecting guardian of his wandering years, and the testimony of their fruition in the years which were yet to come. Such an experience, too, could not have failed to have been Newton's, when the idea of universal gravitation first flashed across his mind, and he realized the subtle bond of connexion by which planets and suns were linked together, and formed into one vast material system. Like Kepler, he must have been assured then, if he did not exclaim, 'O God, I am thinking Thy thoughts after Thee!' Such an experience, once more, Words-worth declared to have been his when, returning home from a night of merriment, 'the morning rose in memorable pomp', glorious as e'er he had beheld, 'and the solid mountains shone, bright as the clouds, grain-tinctured, drenched in empyrean light', and 'in the meadows and the lower grounds was all the sweetness of a common dawn'. Is it surprising that 'to the brim' his heart was full, that, though he made no vows, vows were yet made for him; and that he felt himself then a 'dedicated spirit';—felt himself, in other words, consecrated to a service in which it was bliss to participate.

These, I repeat, were great moments of spiritual or religious experience. But we should fail utterly to appreciate their significance were we to set them down as abnormal episodes, as phases of consciousness having no parallel in the humbler lives of us lesser men and women. The world has had, indeed, and can have, only one Plato. Yet have not countless numbers of us been taught, as he was, at some time or another, how calmly and courageously pain and suffering can be borne, and with what firm trust in divine beneficence death can be faced, by those to whom he has been but little more than a name? The world has had, and can have, only one Dante; but innumerable lives have scanned the heights of duty, and known the sacredness of things divine, through coming under the influence of a love such as that which hallowed his. The world has had, and can have, only one Newton. But many and many a 'lad of parts', after struggling manfully with the impediments and difficulties that have stood in the way of his acquiring the rudiments of intellectual culture, has felt that self-same thrill of joy when some scientific generalization has at last become clear to him, and he is enabled for the first time to grasp one of the root principles on which the constitution of things is based. The world has had, and can have, only one Wordsworth; but who would have repudiated more vehemently than he the notion that he had any title to assert of himself peculiar privilege, or any monopoly of that conscious kinship with the majesty, the loveliness and the serenity of our natural environment, which formed the theme and burden of his greatest poetry? Rather was his message precisely the opposite:

"There's not a man
That lives, who hath not known his godlike hours,
And feels not what an empire we inherit
As natural beings in the strength of nature."

No; great moments of spiritual experience are in no sense reserved for the comparatively rare and lofty souls that lead the march of human progress; such moments come no less to the men and women who make up the community of what George Eliot was in the habit of describing as that of "the commonplace people". The fact is, I venture to assert, that well-nigh every serious and reflective mind amongst us could tell of moments, not indeed of ecstatic exaltation of the mystic type, but of calm rational insight into the spiritual meaning of existence, when he has been conscious of a revelation or filled with an enthusiasm the import of which has been to him infinitely precious, and concerning which he is persuaded it was no phantom of unreality, no delusion from which in his lower moods of habitual perception he was fortunate enough to escape. Call it reason, call it insight, call it inspiration, whatever it be that enables us thus to grasp the deeper significance of the world without and the world within, it engenders the irresistible conviction that the human knower is not alone in knowing the facts of nature, that the human heart is not alone in the love it feels, that the human will is not alone in striving for the good which it reveres. And that surely is what we mean by God—a consciousness that knows all that we cannot know, that loves beyond our power of loving, that 'realizes' the good where our faltering efforts fail.

These intervals of spiritual discernment are, I surmise, far more numerous than we are wont to suspect, for wise men do not make them themes of ordinary conversation or disclose them as topics of debate. Yet, still, for most of us, immersed as we are in the incidents of daily routine, it is only, it has to be confessed,

> " In a season of calm weather
> Though inland far we be,
> Our souls have sight of that immortal sea
> Which brought us hither";

and, in our duller moods, the revelations fade into those of common day, and we are apt to let them slip into the dim background of consciousness. In a passage of austere and singular beauty, Newman spoke of the unequivocable way in which physical nature appeals to the senses. "But", he added, "the phenomena which are the basis of morals and religion have nothing of this luminous evidence. Instead of being obtruded upon our notice, so that we cannot possibly overlook them, they are the dictates either of conscience or of faith. They are faint shadows and tracings, certain indeed, but delicate, fragile, and almost evanescent, which the mind recognizes at one time, not at another,—discerns when it is calm, loses when it is in agitation. The reflection of sky and mountains in the lake is a proof that the sky and mountains are around it, but the twilight, or the mist, or the sudden storm hurries away the beautiful image, which leaves behind it no memorial of what it was. Something like this are the intimations of faith, as they present themselves to individual minds."

Newman was here giving utterance in his own way to what must be acknowledged as very generally characteristic of religious experience. For most of us, as Henry Sidgwick once said, "the revealing visions come and go"; when they come we are assured that we *know*; but in the intervals we pass through states of hesitation and misgiving, and "in which we can only struggle to hold the conviction that

> 'Power is with us in the night
> Which makes the darkness and the light,
> And dwells not in the light alone'."

Is not that, however, a conviction worth attaining? For, after all, the attitude of implicit *trust* in the goodness of the Power that guides the course of events is an essential ingredient of the developed religious consciousness; and it may well be that, if we are fully to realize what it is thus to *trust*, we needs must pass through seasons when clouds darken our horizon and the Divine is screened from our view. It may legitimately be questioned whether the kind of certainty which belief in an infallible Church engenders is faith in all its purity. And, on the other hand, the spirit of modest, humble, open-hearted doubt, which trusts in spite of darkness, in spite of uncertainty, if it is not faith in its purity, borders closely upon it.

6. Whoever takes a sufficiently wide glance at the course of human history cannot fail to be struck with a characteristic which it is constantly illustrating,— the surprising manner, namely, in which truths are anticipated and acted upon generations before they are rationally formulated or scientifically established. An interesting instance of what I mean came to light during the years of the Great War. For centuries the Catholic Church had been applying in the Confessional a method of psycho-therapeutics which recent research has shown to be based on sound psychological principles, and which was the means, in hospital practice, of curing hundreds of cases of mental disorder, occasioned by what was gone through in the trenches and on the battlefield. But instances abound and will occur to everybody. Men sowed fields and reaped harvests before they had any notions of the principles of agriculture; they sailed ships before navigation became a science; they used wheels and pulleys long before any system of mechanics was propounded;

they even predicted solar eclipses ages before the
beginnings of what can be called astronomy. Just as
in the animal world instinct precedes intelligence,
and guides living creatures where they would otherwise be hopelessly baffled in the struggle for existence,
so in the human world men are led by a way they
know not to a premonition of truths which, long subsequently, reason confirms. "When we regard the development of living forms as a continuous whole, we are
forced", wrote James Ward, "to recognize, as immin-
ent and operative throughout it, a sort of unscientific
trustfulness, that from the very first seems to have
been engrained in all living things"; and he compared
this trustfulness to the faith of Abraham who, "when
he was called to go out into a place which he should
after receive for an inheritance, obeyed and went out,
not knowing whither he went".[1]

In all spheres of human experience this 'unscientific trustfulness' is exhibited, but pre-eminently in that
experience we have been calling religious. Even in
its rudimentary stages men get already accustomed
to the facts of self-control, self-denial, self-sacrifice,
forgiveness of sins and atonement; men act and behave
as though there were a life after death centuries
before they begin to discuss its possibility or embark
upon speculations about it. Religious ideas, such
as those of the Fatherhood of God, of the brotherhood of man, and of the future life, were certainly
not originally reached by a strictly logical process of
reasoning. But then that is true of virtually all the
ideas by which human life is guided. Even the scientist

[1] *The Realm of Ends*, p. 416.

never rests content with what he can logically justify. On the basis of a number of ascertained facts he constructs hypotheses or theories such as those of the conservation of energy, evolution, or relativity; and in these theories he more or less firmly believes or has faith; from the facts which he knows with certainty his mind is impelled to believe in what he cannot be said to know with like certainty. Yet to draw in this case a hard-and-fast line between knowing and believing would be psychologically altogether unwarranted. In framing a theory or hypothesis the scientific man is no less intellectually active, no less exercising his facility of knowing, than in observing particular facts. It is true that religious faith differs in important respects from scientific belief. In particular, its domain is largely that of practice, whereas scientific beliefs are, as a rule, essentially and primarily theoretic in their bearing. The religious man not only believes in God, but finds satisfaction in that belief; he not only affirms the reality of religious values but is assured that they have been the source of whatever has been best in him and in his deeds. Consequently, the test of religious faith lies, it is often claimed, in the kind of conduct which it inspires, and in the contribution which it makes to human well-being. "Life", it is urged, "is primarily active, not contemplative; and thus it is only in striving for what is good that we learn what is true; only as interested in the 'what for' that we inquire about the 'what'."[1] Be it so; but, after all, the difference is not really a fundamental difference. For, in the long run, the practical

[1] James Ward, *op. cit.*, p. 419.

test is a test determined by the intellect. The intellect surveys, guides and judges what conscience is said to enjoin. Not only so. Practical conduct is no blind acting; it is essentially intelligent acting, acting in which rational discernment has been from first to last the predominant factor. Without intelligent discernment, without previous knowledge, practice simply amounts to nothing. The religious man may, indeed, justifiably testify to what his religion has meant for him; how it has moulded the course of his life, sustained him in all his efforts, and been to him a source of strength in the pursuit of worthy ends. And it is, undoubtedly, in that way that religious ideas have been probed and tested prior to the direction upon them of critical scrutiny. They take shape, it is true, in a framework of imagery,—how else could they take shape at all?—and nothing is easier than for a merely iconoclastic mind to shatter the framework and cover its contents with the débris. Such treatment is parallel to the way in which Cromwell and his Ironsides dealt with the medieval art of former times which they could neither appreciate nor understand. That is, indeed, but poor and fruitless criticism which would obliterate the essence of what is taken to be spiritually discerned because, forsooth, it can find expression only in frail and imperfect forms. The fact is, religious experience has no other medium at its disposal wherewith to express itself than that of imagery and metaphor; its truth *must* be 'embodied in a tale', if it is to 'enter in at lowly doors'. This medium may and, of course, does become more refined and appropriate with the lapse of time; but it was employed by Denison Maurice, Caird and Martineau no less than by St. Augustine or John Wesley.

There is, then, no radical antithesis between faith and knowledge. It is obvious that faith involves some kind of knowing, and that were we to descend below a certain level of intelligence to talk of 'faith' would be meaningless. Faith clearly cannot be said to be destitute of thought. Even in the lower sense of mere supposition, of what Plato called opinion (δόξα), it is mainly, if not wholly, an imperfectly developed intellectual process. And, in that more definite and personal form which we have been considering, faith is only possible as being based on ideas which are obtained only through the intellect. Faith is, if you will, implicit reason, reason working with ideas or concepts which it has obtained through reflexion upon what is offered in experience, but which it has not sought to verify scientifically, or which, it may be, cannot be thus verified. And to me it seems helpful, in this context, to bear in mind that faith, so conceived, is not peculiar to the sphere of religion, but that down the ages through its agency, so understood, there has been vouchsafed to men an *Ahnung*, a presentiment, of truths which reason, in the more specific sense, can acquire only as an outcome of arduous labour, and "when the evening twilight begins to fall".[1]

[1] In a sense, as has often been pointed out, science itself ultimately rests upon a species of faith. It proceeds on the supposition that the world of facts is intellectually coherent, but this supposition must remain unproven, simply because the whole of existence has not been scientifically explored.

V

THE COSMOLOGICAL ARGUMENT

I HAVE striven to show how far reason can carry us when we look upon it as being involved in all our experiences, and as at the root of all intelligent belief. The methods of knowing must, and, of course, do, depend upon the material upon which it is engaged; but these differences of method are, after all, relatively superficial, because fundamentally there is only one way of knowing. Wise men and simple, scientific and unscientific, contemplative and practical, all employ ultimately the same means of ascertaining the truth or falsity of what seems to be offered in experience, and of determining what are the actual facts. They all employ thought or reason, and thought or reason has invariably its own way of working. In other words, reason is not an activity of mind that first comes into operation with the advent of the scientist or the philosopher; on the contrary, science and philosophy are only possible on the basis of what thought or reason has already achieved in the ordinary walks of life. Science, as T. H. Huxley once remarked, is but systematized and organized common-sense; and the same may be said to be true of philosophy. In point of fact, the way in which rational thought does its work is exemplified in every judgment which common, sense makes, and in every complete sentence, spoken or written, by which such judgment is expressed. Every judgment is, in short, at once analytic and synthetic,—analytic because it breaks up or sunders what in presentative experience is given in conjunction; synthetic because it unites these discriminated elements in a way in which they are not at first seen to be united, and by so doing enriches the so-called subject of the judgment and specializes the generality which forms its predicate. Common-sense knowledge, then, advancing by a series of judgments, exhibits a twofold mode of progress,—on the one hand, an ever-increasing number of recognized distinctions; and, on the other hand, an ever-increasing richness and fullness of the individual concrete objects into which the whole has been differentiated.

But, although the method of reason is throughout fundamentally the same in kind, yet obviously that method may more or less clearly or confusedly, more or less adequately or inadequately, more or less exactly or crudely, be employed. And herein lies the essential difference between scientific and common-sense thinking. The scientific man is continually seeking to bring to light in reference to any given body of facts a general principle which they exemplify, and to show that any newly discovered relevant facts likewise exemplify what he takes to be the general principle in question. He views, that is to say, each particular fact as an instance of a law. Not only so. The scientific investigator carries with him, well-nigh from the start, a conception of what he takes the law in question to be. He has his own hypothesis, which may indeed turn out to be in need of modification or even to be ill-founded; but there is no science, in the strict sense, until there is a hypothesis on its trial. It is not a mere collection of facts, however similar, that constitutes a science, but the way in which those facts are dealt with.

And, if I mistake not, the relation in which philosophical investigation stands to religious thought and reflexion is, in many ways, similar to that in which science stands to common-sense thinking generally. The religious man, if his religion be not a mere matter of routine or tradition, has convinced himself that experience, taken in the wider sense, exhibits principles which a mere mechanism would leave inexplicable; he is virtually affirming that the intelligible aspect of the universe is the most striking aspect of it which he can contemplate, that the universe seems to him singularly purposive and in its higher reaches to display a moral order or structure, in short that it brings him into relationship with a supreme and all-ruling Mind. Moreover, he will point to the value which genuine devotion to a Being spiritually perfect has been to countless generations of sincere and worthy lives, and urge this as a rational ground for his belief. "If we are honest with ourselves", wrote T. H. Green, in an impressive passage, "we shall admit that something best called faith, a prevailing conviction of our presence to God and his to us, of his gracious mind towards us, . . . has been the source of whatever has been best in us and in our deeds. If we have enough experience and sympathy to interpret fairly the life of the world around us, we shall admit that faith of this sort is the salt of the earth. Through it, below the surface of circumstance and custom, humanity is being renewed day by day; and, unless our heart is sealed by selfishness and sophistry, though we may not consciously share in the process, there will be men and times that make us reverentially feel its reality. Who can hear an unargumentative and unrhetorical Christian minister appeal to his people to cleanse their hearts and to help each other as sons of God in Christ, without feeling that he touches the deepest and strongest spring of noble conduct in mankind?"[1]

Such, then, are some of the ways in which ordinary common-sense reflexion contrives to make manifest the rational grounds of religious belief. The fact is that few thoughtful persons, however persuaded they may be of the immediateness of religious experience, or of the intuitive certainty of its contents, are satisfied to leave the matter there. They recognize that experience of whatsoever kind may be, and often is, wrongly interpreted by the experient; and that, although the experient may be strongly convinced of the truth of his interpretation, yet his conviction may prove to be illusory. They are, therefore, constantly making efforts to justify the faith that is in them; and it is, indeed, notorious that all down the ages theologians have been intent upon showing that rational proof can be furnished of the cardinal principles of religious belief. Now, philosophical

[1] *Works*, vol. iii, p. 258-9.

inquiry may legitimately enough be said to be an endeavour to carry on that reflective work with greater precision and with greater exactitude. It does not, of course, follow that, after having definitely formulated the claims which the religious consciousness makes on reality, it is the business of philosophy to substantiate those claims as they stand, or indeed to substantiate them at all. The business of philosophy is to explicate and examine them, to ascertain whether they will stand the test of critical examination. Moreover, the philosopher has to keep in view a consideration which the religious man is apt to ignore, that the postulates of religious experience can only be valid if they are consistent with the presuppositions on which experience in its totality rests.

I propose in the present lecture to inquire as to what can be said from a philosophical point of view about a mode of reasoning that has, in one form or another, been widely prevalent in religious and theological thought, and which in a more or less loose way largely influences popular reflexion. Let us see what light philosophical scrutiny can throw upon what is in truth one of the two oldest of the arguments advanced in proof of the existence of God.

1. This argument may, in a concise fashion, be stated thus. Starting from an undeniable deliverance of experience,—namely, that there are such entities as existing things and events,—it is noted that these existing things and events reveal themselves, even on the most cursory inspection, to be contingent in character,—that is to say, as not being there in virtue of any intrinsic necessity of their own. Such necessity

as appertains to them is relative and hypothetical. We can say that if the event C be given the event D necessarily follows. The occurrence of the event D is, in other words, only conditionally necessary—necessary in the sense that it is constrained. In virtue of its own character merely, and apart from the existence of the event C, this event D would not exist. And similarly, of course, in regard to the event C; its existence is only conditionally necessary on the occurrence of an event B; and, again, the existence of the event B is only conditionally necessary on the occurrence of an event A, and so on *ad indefinitum*. Throughout nature we find, accordingly, only this conditional necessity; nothing happens there except as a consequence of something else happening. And, if this be true of all that nature contains, it must likewise be true of nature in its entirety. In the long run, therefore, the existence of nature must depend upon a Being whose existence is intrinsically or unconditionally necessary,—a Being, that is to say, that is not dependent for its existence upon the prior existence of something else. Or, to bring out the contention in another way, just as in the realm of knowledge we cannot go on indefinitely giving reasons for propositions that we hold to be true, but must come in the end to propositions that are self-evident, or contain within themselves their own justification,[1] so in the realm of existence we cannot be condemned forever to the mere treadmill exercise of an indefinite regress; but must, presuming,

---

[1] We cannot, for example, prove, in the strict sense, the truth of the law of contradiction. The only proof we can offer is that if it is not true there is nothing else that is true.

of course, that our intellectual powers are adequate to the task, come ultimately upon a reality that is there, so to speak, in its own right, the conception of which does not need the conception of something else upon which it is dependent.

2. I do not think that the argument I have thus sketched is so entirely devoid of justification as Kant, in the *Critique of Pure Reason*, took it to be; and I shall presently try to show what amount of justification may legitimately be ascribed to it. But, meanwhile, I want to dwell upon a form of the argument in which use is made of the principle of causality which does seem to me open to serious criticism.

Even so able and acute a theologian as Robert Flint spent endless pains to make good the contention that, because every particular fact in the universe reveals mutability stamped upon it, and must be treated as an event dependent upon a preceding event, therefore the universe as a whole must be an event or an effect in the same sense. But the premisses simply do not warrant that conclusion. It does not follow that because the notion of cause and effect is applicable to existent parts of the universe it is likewise applicable to the universe in its entirety, or as a whole.

It has long been recognized in philosophical discussions of the subject that the idea of creation, as an event occurring at a specific date in the past, in consequence of a fiat on the part of the Deity, is beset with numerous difficulties and inconsistencies. The universe, so frequently the cosmological argument has been set out as implying, cannot always have been in existence; for, in that case, we should be compelled to acknowledge that, at any assigned moment of time, an infinite time had actually been completed, and that would be a contradiction in terms. The universe must, therefore, have had a beginning; and consequently we are constrained to postulate a 'First Cause'. It needs, however, but little philosophy to detect some of the manifest incongruities involved in this mode of reasoning. For instance, the awkward question at once arises—What induced the beginner to begin and to begin just then? Can we intelligibly conceive of a Deity quiescent for ages, and then, once upon a time, being suddenly stimulated to call a universe into being?

But I desire rather to go to what seems to me the root of the matter, and to inquire whether we are at all entitled to distinguish two types of causality,— causality such as is manifested in the realm of material nature and causality as it is taken to be manifested in what I may call for the moment volitions. For it is to be observed that the notion of a 'first cause' or a 'free cause' is by no means confined to the case of God's activity. To man as a self-conscious agent the notion is likewise applied, indicating, I take it, that, though a conscious subject is the cause of his actions, he is, nevertheless, not to be regarded as determined after the fashion which is assumed to hold within the realm of the objective facts of which he is cognizant. And what I wish now to ask is whether we are really justified in thus employing the term 'cause' when its special significance is regarded as being not unique but two-fold, whether we are justified in viewing the two cases, objective connexion of events and relation of the subject to his activity, as being on the same level. I shall venture to urge that we are not.

On considering the objective connexion of material events we may be led to see that the notion of causal relation is a way in which we express but one aspect of the connexions assumed to hold among the events contemplated by us. It is, so to speak, an abstract expression which brings into prominence one portion only of what is involved in our notion of objective fact, but the meaning of which cannot be satisfactorily brought out so long as we isolate that portion. When we say that two events are causally connected we mean that the sequent event is, as regards time and manner of occurrence, determined by the first. And, for practical purposes, we rarely look beyond this special form of connexion, in which events are thrown into series of antecedents and dependent consequents. But it is evident that no antecedent in such a series can be other than an event; and that, if the principle of causal connexion be universal in import, each cause is, at the same time, rightly to be conceived as an effect or consequent. A 'first cause' which is an event or a 'free cause' which is an event must, then, equally contradict the very notion of causal relation with which we are proceeding. Causality as a relation is taken, that is to say, in a one-sided fashion unless we keep both constituents of the notion in view. Every cause is at the same time an effect; and, although we practically incline to regard the cause as indeterminate in contrast to the determinateness of the effect, it is evident that the cause is just as determinate as the effect assumed to depend upon it. Accordingly, there is involved in the thought of causal connexion the view of natural events as forming parts of a complete system, each part being determined by the way in which it stands to other parts of the system. It is, then, illegitimate to place in the relation of cause and effect entities which, on whatsoever ground, we are compelled to regard as not forming parts of one and the same system. And a certain identity in essential nature of the connected entities is necessarily involved in their forming parts of one and the same system.

Furthermore, the principle of causal relations implies, in truth, the additional thought that the facts or events thus connected are, or conceivably might be, *objects* for intelligence, and that the system which they form is a system of *objects* for intelligence. It is, in fact, through the notion of a causally interconnected system that we give precision to the thought of an *objective* world as such. We have, then, a ready means of determining a limit to the application of the notion of cause. Wherever the entities under consideration cannot be regarded as *objects*, but can be construed or interpreted only in a way other than that which is appropriate in the case of objects, there the application of the thought of causal nexus is illegitimate. Now, we have previously seen that it *is* inconsequent first of all to distinguish between subject and object, and then, having made that distinction, to forthwith treat the knowing subject as being, in like manner, one of the objects of the known objective world.[1] The whole nature of mental life, what gives it significance at all, is just that which in no way presents

[1] See *supra*, p. 165.

itself to us as one object amongst others. Accordingly, however strange it may appear at first sight, we are driven to the conclusion that, in whatsoever manner we are to designate the relation between a conscious subject and his actions, the relation is not that recognized by us as obtaining between an objective cause and its objective effect.

3. The most resolute of all the attempts which have been made to conceive of God as the 'First Cause' is, I apprehend, decidedly that of Dr. Martineau, in his great work *A Study of Religion*. Two lines of reflexion are there relied upon as leading irresistibly to the conviction that "the universe which includes and folds us round is the Life-dwelling of an Eternal Mind." The one is the metaphysical argument from our own inalienable experience of ourselves as causes and voluntary agents to the conception of God as will and the source of power; and the other the moral argument which proceeds from the experience of conscience in ourselves to the conception of God as the source of moral ideals. We are concerned, at present, only with the former of these.

This argument proceeds from an analysis of the act of perception, which gives us, it is maintained, simultaneous knowledge of a subject and of an object. Perception is not, however, to be identified with mere passive receptivity. Not until the conscious being encounters some obstacle, not until resistance is offered to its activity and an effort made to overcome such resistance, not until then does the act of perception really take place. In this collision two pairs of opposites are at once revealed,—the self *here* and the not-self *there*, personal causation and extra-personal causation; these are recognized together, and are, at the same time, discriminated from one another. The not-self is disclosed to us as the reality of an external world, not as something constructed by the mind's own act, but as something which, while apprehended by the mind, is independent of it. It is true, so Martineau was prepared to admit, that we are directly aware only of the effects, the phenomenal appearances, which this external world produces in our minds; but, he urged, in and along with the perception of these presentations we instinctively ascribe them to a cause, to an operating force. That every phenomenon must have a cause or be the expression of some power is an immediate intuition of human intelligence, and an intuition we are bound to trust at the peril of finding otherwise our so-called knowledge dissipating itself into a dream. Once suppose that we are deceived when thought assures us that we are stationed in an infinitude of space, through every region of which the principles of mathematics are valid, once concede that we err when we conceive that in such space a vast network of dynamic forces is at work, and the whole fabric of what we take to be scientific knowledge will collapse into a heap of ruins. Space and time, and within them causal potencies, must, therefore, assuredly *be*; and our ideas of these, although not given *by* experience, must nevertheless be inherent in our mental constitution. There can be no higher authentication for anything than that we are obliged to think it.

The next step Martineau took by adopting the contention of Berkeley that the only actual experience we have of causation and of the exertion of force is that which we find in ourselves. The experience of causation in ourselves is the birthplace of all knowledge of and reflexion upon causation elsewhere; we are constrained by an inevitable necessity of thought to believe that there can be no causation other than voluntary causation, that, in the long run, cause and will mean the same thing. This belief Martineau conceived to be involved in even the primitive consciousness; and it is, he urged, a belief which physical science is constantly engaged in elaborating. For the scientist the world is, in truth, not a scene of things but an assemblage of powers. "Instead of each concrete object appearing as a substantive thing with many functions, each *function* appears as *one power* contributing to constitute many things: *it* is the *real*, they are but the *show-place*. The individual which presses upon sense and imagination is but the phenomenal meeting-point, the transient rendez-vous of permanent and universal powers, which are for ever engaged in building and rebuilding the cosmos."[1] And, being conscious of ourselves as exerting power or putting forth energy, we are constrained to think of the vast forces or modes of energy in nature as having been "put forth" or "planted out" in space by the supreme Mind. Martineau conceived space to be an eternal condition of the divine activity, an uncreated counterpart of God's being. As such, it constitutes the frame-work for all the 'happenings' or events which it is the business of science to sort into groups, and summarize in those formulae of

[1] *A Study of Religion*, 1st ed., vol. i, p. 251.

uniform occurrences which are described as 'laws'. But to the occurrences themselves no causation attaches; they are but the expressions of phases of power under various combinations of circumstances; and scientists ought not to speak of *them* as causes. Not only so. While the element of power is an essential ingredient of a cause, it does not of itself constitute one. More is demanded of a cause than that it should *do* something; it must be the determinant of a specific change, of *this* rather than *that*, and involves choice between two or more alternative directions of activity. And that is precisely what we mean by will or deliberate purpose. Consequently, since volition or will is the essence of what we are aware of in ourselves as personality, we are justified in carrying back the occurrences of nature to the being of a supreme Personality,—a Personality which religious thought has conceived under the name of God.

Despite the forcible manner in which Dr. Martineau supported the position just outlined, his argumentation breaks down, I think, when critically inspected.

In the first place, it is based on a conception of human volition or will which I can only describe as essentially unpsychological and indefensible. Too often we are tempted to speak of the will as though it were "a central power-installation somewhere in the depths of our personality, which can be connected up with a pump or a saw or any other machine we may desire to use".[1] But the will is not, any more than the intellect, an engine which produces certain results. Recall, once more, the crucial difference which

[1] *Cf.* R. G. Collingwood, *Religion and Philosophy*, p. 103.

we have seen to subsist between an *object* and the *knowledge or consciousness of an object*; and the reason why we found it to be erroneous to regard the latter as itself an object.[1] In a like manner and for a like reason, I would now insist that there is a radical difference between what we call 'energy' or 'force' and the consciousness of energy or force; and that it is a fatal mistake to take for granted, as, indeed, is frequently taken for granted, that the consciousness of energy or force must itself be a mode of force or energy. It is certainly true that in many acts of willing, though by no means in all, we are conscious of what we call exerting energy or effort, but the energy or effort we are thus aware of is no less objective in character than is the colour of a thing of which we are aware in an act of visual perception. Whoever recognizes the distinction between a red colour and the act of apprehending it is bound in consistency likewise to recognize the distinction between what we call energy or effort and the act of apprehending it; and whoever questions the legitimacy of describing a red colour as a mental fact is equally entitled to question the legitimacy of describing energy or effort as a mental fact. In other words, the latter may well be, and I think is, a bodily fact.[2] If the attempt be seriously made to think out what can be meant by a 'putting forth' of energy or force on the part of a

[1] See *supra*, p. 66 *sqq.*

[2] That it is a bodily fact in a great number of cases is beyond dispute; the only question is whether it is not so in all. In this connexion I may perhaps be allowed to refer to my papers on "The Nature of Willing" (*Proceedings of Aristotelian Society*, N.S., vol. xiii, 1913) and on "The Dynamic Aspect of Nature" (*ibid.*, vol. xxv, 1925).

mind, it will be found that no intelligible notion can be formed of any such operation. And the attempt will result in failure because the conception of energy or force is really applicable only to physical events or occurrences; energy or force is explicable only in terms of mass and velocity. To picture mental activity as identical in kind with physical activity is virtually to picture consciousness after the fashion of material mechanism. Martineau had, of course, no intention of doing anything of the sort. He conceived that by means of the notion of self-conscious will, deliberately selecting among alternatives, the thought of mechanical energy or force had been completely transformed. So far, however, as the idea of force or energy had been incorporated in the notion of will there had been, in truth, no such transformation.

In the second place, even were we to grant that the human will is rightly regarded as a mode of exerting power or of expending force, it is clear that in a most fundamental respect the analogy drawn between the human will and the divine breaks down. For admittedly the human will operates with borrowed energy and a vast tissue of conditions; it compasses its ends by adjusting a mechanism which is already there for the accomplishment of such ends, and out of its own inner resources it adds not one atom to the contents of nature. The divine Will, on the other hand, draws, according to the theory, upon nothing but itself; it is itself the huge reservoir or storehouse from which the whole material of the world emanates. We shall have, therefore, radically to change our notion of Will if it is to be equal to the demands which are thus required of it; and, when we have done so, it would surely be evident that we are landed with the notion of something absolutely different from what we are familiar with under the name of volition. The question would then confront us whether the conception of God as a vast source of energy which is being perpetually projected into space is compatible with the conception of God as a mental life or spiritual personality.

In the third place, it is worth pointing out that the contrast which Martineau drew between the *immanence* of God in material nature and God's *transcendence* in respect to our human personalities leads to a surprising and perplexing consequence, which Martineau himself hardly seems to have realized. However independent and self-poised the finite mind may be supposed to be, one thing, at least, is certain,—it did not create or call into being its own animal body. And over the processes of that bodily structure it has throughout only a very limited and partial control; they go on, for the most part, without its knowledge or supervision. Now, the elements of the bodily structure belong, of course, to the material world; and, free as man may be to choose his own line of conduct, he can only carry out his resolves in so far as, through the instrumentality of his bodily organism, he brings about a change in the world around him. Such changes may tend either to the furthering or to the impeding of the 'realization' of that ideal good towards which the divine agency is *ex hypothesi* working. Consider, then, those changes initiated by man that result in evil and vice. We are driven to this momentous conclusion, that the Will of God,—admittedly a self-conscious, rational will,—which constitutes the reality of the physical universe, is of such a nature that it lends itself to the will of the human wrong-doer, becomes, so to speak, subordinate to the latter in order to give 'realization' to a state of things which is iniquitous and unworthy, and contrary to what it itself is striving to bring about in the world. Such a position it is extraordinarily difficult to render so much as thinkable.

4. The idea of creation as an event which occurred at a definite date in the past calls, then, to be unhesitatingly rejected. One thing at least which those who speak of the world as a 'creation' are intending to express is its dependence upon God. But such dependence cannot obviously be causal dependence in the strict sense of that phrase. For if it were, it would imply either a change in something already existing other than God, or else a change in God Himself, whereby from a condition of non-creativeness God passed into one of creativeness. And each of these alternatives is clearly contradictory.

If the notion of 'creation' is to be sustained at all it can only be in the sense of continuous creation, of a constant dependence of the world on the supreme Being. "In truth", wrote Ulrici, a prominent defender of theism in the latter half of the nineteenth century, "God is not *first* God and *then* creator of the world, but *as* God He is creator, and only *as* creator of the world is He God."[1] It has been suggested that a faint analogy to what is here meant may be discerned in what we are wont to style creations of genius. The things of beauty which the artist or poet produces

[1] *Gott und Welt*, p. 532.

we are accustomed to look upon as the spontaneous output of a free spirit that embodies itself in its work, and, so to speak, lives in it. Yet the artist is still distinct from it, and it from him; even in the midst of his activity, he is assured that it is working itself out, that he is finding himself expressed in it.[1] Such a conception is, it is true, at a wide remove from the popular idea of the world being created out of nothing. But, then, rightly or wrongly, the term 'creation' has been used to express various conceptions of very different import. Even Spinoza and Hegel speak of 'creation' when they really mean 'emanation'. All things, on their view, 'flow' or 'proceed' from God, so that all finite entities, although at different removes from the primitive essence, are part and parcel of the divine Being.

It should, however, be borne in mind that in the oldest form of the cosmological argument, or the argument *a contingentia mundi*, that which we find in the writings of Aristotle, God was not represented as the Creator of the universe, even in the sense in which creation is understood as continuous creation. When Aristotle spoke of the "Unmoved Mover" as the primary cause (αἴτιον), he meant by 'cause', in this context, the ultimate principle or ground (ἀρχή) of all that is. He did not argue to the existence of God from the supposed necessity of a *prius* to the temporal series. On the contrary, his contention was that a world of ceaseless change is only explicable when it is regarded as maintained by and dependent upon one supreme unchanging Being, whose constant

[1] James Ward, *The Realm of Ends*, p. 239.

M

presence educes the series of 'forms' latent in the 'matter' of the universe into actual manifestation. The Deity is not himself compounded, as mutable things are, of 'matter' and 'form'; his individuality is one of pure 'form' or 'actuality,' and has behind it no gradual process of development. This prime Mover, this pure Form, stationed outside of and transcending the realm of the mutable, produces movement or change in that realm not by motion in himself but after the manner in which the good or the beautiful incites change of emotion or desire (ὄρεξις) on the part of finite minds. The series of transitions in nature originate from, or express, that is to say, a certain striving of the changeable towards the perfect model of the unchanging. But the point on which I would here lay stress is that Aristotle, and indeed the Greek philosophers generally, looked upon the orderly realm of natural processes as having neither beginning nor end. The cosmos, the world of generation, they conceived to be no less everlasting than God on whom it depends; in other words, the changeable no less than the changeless is an ultimate component of Reality as a whole.[1]

Perhaps, indeed, the Greek thinkers recognized more clearly than we are apt to do that there are questions which ought never to be asked, because the asking of them involves assumptions which are in truth absurd. For example, it is nonsense to ask how

[1] This contention occasioned no little trouble to the scholastic Aristotelians. St. Thomas, who was constrained to admit, as being a truth vouched by revelation, that the world was actually brought into existence a few thousand years before his own time, yet strenuously denied that the truth of the doctrine of creation could be philosophically demonstrated.

Reality itself came to be, because any 'coming to be' implies the being of reality. It is only within the realm of Reality that anything can either come to be or cease to be. And so, too, the notion of the coming to be of becoming may turn out, when scrutinized, to be an unintelligible notion. Certainly, if it is permissible to conceive of space as the uncreated counterpart of God's being,[1] I can find no reason why the matter which fills space should not likewise be conceived as an uncreated counterpart of God's being. And this, I take it, was virtually what Bergson was concerned to substantiate by his masterly and effective criticism of the idea of Nothing (*l'idée de néant*).[2] He brings into clear relief how existence comes to appear for us as though it were a conquest over nought. We say to ourselves that there might conceivably be 'nothing', and then wonder how there comes to be something. Or, if something has always existed, 'nothing' must have subserved as its substratum or receptacle, and is, therefore, eternally prior. In short, we cannot rid ourselves of the notion that being is superimposed on 'nothing', and that in the representation of 'nothing' *less* is contained than in that of something. But this idea of Nothing, in the sense in which we take it when we oppose it to that of existence, is, as Bergson conclusively shows, a pseudo-idea, and the problems which are raised round it are pseudo-problems. In the field of actual experience we can, it is true, annihilate particular objects, but we can do so only by substituting for them other objects. And if annihilation signifies invariably substitution, then

[1] See *supra*, p. 170.   [2] *L'Évolution Créatice*, p. 298 *sqq.*

the thought of an 'annihilation of everything' is no less absurd than that of a square circle. It implies, that is to say, a downright contradiction, because the operation would consist in destroying the very condition which renders an act of destruction possible.

5. Let me, then, now try to bring out what I conceive to be the essential truth which the cosmological argument, when rightly stated, establishes. The gist of the argument may be expressed thus: Acknowledging, as we cannot help doing, the existence of the world of nature, we are logically driven to acknowledge that there is real existence beyond nature, unless, indeed, we are prepared to rest in an ultimate inexplicability, and to relinquish the attempt to frame any intelligible conception of nature at all.[1] First of all, let us be clear as to what exactly these alternatives mean. The scientific investigator, within the field of his own special science, is doubtless justified in insisting that it is not his business to 'explain' the facts of nature, in the sense, that is, of the term 'explanation' which is here in question. He is justified in maintaining that his function has been fulfilled if he has succeeded in discovering *within nature* the causes or conditions that occasion the specific events with which he happens to be concerned. But it is quite another matter to allege that a position of this kind either is or can be the final word of a *philosophy* of nature. Whoever supposes it to be the final word is virtually implying that there is just no reason why the constituents of nature are as they are, why there

---

[1] Understanding by 'nature' in this context the sum of inter-related objects with which natural science is concerned. *Cf. supra*, p. 164.

are so many different kinds of them, or why they have the specific characteristics they are found to have, except, indeed, the 'reason' which is, in truth, no reason, that such 'happens to be the case'. He is implying, in other words, that there might just as well have been no world at all, or a world totally other than the actual one. And this means, as Professor Taylor has ably argued, that we are simply acquiescing in unexplained 'brute fact', not because in the present state of our knowledge we can do no otherwise, but on the ground that there is not and cannot be any explanation,—on the ground, that is to say, that unintelligible mystery subsists at the very core of reality.[1]

And why not, it may possibly be asked? May not unintelligible mystery be precisely what is at the core of reality? It is, I take it, sufficient to answer that the acceptance of such a position would undermine the very principle upon which scientific research invariably proceeds. Throughout its history, it has been tacitly assumed that reality *is* intelligible, that wherever we come upon what, in the light of our present knowledge, we are obliged to accept as mere 'brute fact', there a problem for science is presented, there the scientist is called upon to seek for further explanation. The faith of science is, as Professor Whitehead has put it, the faith that at the base of things we shall not find unintelligible mystery. The conclusion would seem, then, to follow either that the principle which guides

[1] *Cf.* A. E. Taylor's most suggestive contribution, already referred to, on "The Vindication of Religion" to the volume *Essays, Catholic and Critical*, p. 52 *sqq.*

scientific inquiry is deceptive and illusory, or else that nature must be ultimately dependent upon a reality beyond itself, a reality which is self-explanatory. And if the former alternative be dismissed, the latter would seem to be inevitable, because scientific explanation, sufficient though it may be held to be within its own domain, is never exhaustive or complete. Science, in short, is inspired by an ideal which, from the very necessity of the case, it can never itself justify. To put it bluntly, the scientific investigator is impelled incessantly to press into nature in quest of that which is beyond nature.

The objection I have urged against the cruder form of the argument might, it is true, likewise be brought, in a somewhat different setting, against the form of it just indicated. It might, I mean, be contended that, though in accounting for any specific part of nature we are driven to have recourse to showing its dependence upon other parts, and so on indefinitely, yet the aggregate of nature may be self-explanatory, and be the necessarily existent Being upon which the contingent existence of each single event ultimately depends.[1] Or, as the contention has been put by certain modern philosophers, nature may be a system such that, while every part of it, taken singly, is temporal, the whole is eternal, such that, while every part is mutable, the whole is immutable, such that, while

---

[1] "Why", asks Cleanthes, in Hume's *Dialogues concerning Natural Religion*, "why may not the material universe be the necessary existent Being? We dare not affirm that we know all the qualities of matter; and for aught we can determine, it may contain some qualities, which, were they known, would make its non-existence appear as great a contradiction as that twice two is five."

every part is incomplete, the whole is complete. And, in this case, the contrast will be not between nature and that which is beyond nature, but between nature conceived as a whole, and nature conceived, as we are obliged to conceive it, piecemeal and fragmentarily. But here, I think, we are justified in raising the question which Professor Taylor[1] raises, and which goes to the root of the matter, the question, namely, are we entitled to treat 'Nature' as a 'whole' at all? If by 'Nature' be meant simply a vast complex of things and events—and that would seem to be what is usually meant by those who lay stress on this consideration— then, clearly, in virtue of its very structure, it is essentially incomplete and not a self-contained whole. On the contrary, it exhibits everywhere what William James used to call 'ragged edges'. Doubtless, given a certain number of material elements, you can, in a sense, 'explain' the behaviour of any one of them by taking account of its structure, the structure of its correlatives, and the mode of interaction between the latter and it. And so likewise in regard to every one of the elements of the natural world. It will still, however, remain entirely unexplained, and from the data you thus possess entirely inexplicable, why these particular elements should be there at all or why their structure should be what it is and not altogether different. You have got, in short, simply to accept these elements as so much 'brute fact' before your process of scientific 'explanation' can even get under way; and, however extensive your knowledge of so-called 'natural laws,' it will not enable you to

[1] *Essays, Catholic and Critical*, p. 53.

advance a step towards accounting for the present actual state of nature, unless you assume to start with an 'initial' distribution of elements (protons and electrons, or what not) at a certain date in the past, an 'initial' distribution which, as such, is entirely arbitrary. The laws might have been precisely the same; but, had the 'initial' distribution been other than what it was, the actual state of nature to-day would have been different from what it is. As old Dr. Chalmers used to put it, "there are in nature not only laws but collocations"; and by 'collocations' he meant concrete concomitant elements.[1] No doubt, if you could eliminate 'bare fact' altogether, and reduce 'Nature' simply to a concourse of laws, Nature might be conceived as self-explanatory, but obviously that is out of the question; there are no means of conjuring particular existents out of universals. And the more scientific inquirers succeed in finding in Nature a reign of law, the more and not the less baffling becomes the mass of characteristics which they have to ascribe to the ultimate constituents. As Professor Taylor aptly expresses it, "an electron is a much stiffer dose of 'brute' fact than one of Newton's hard impenetrable corpuscles". It would seem, then, that the duality of 'law' and 'fact' does ultimately imply that Nature, understood in the sense I have indicated, is not a self-contained whole, but depends upon a reality that transcends Nature.

[1] In recent times, Emile Meyerson has likewise been insisting that, while the aim of science is the discovery of rationality in things, this ideal is one which can never be completely achieved owing to the presence of residual elements in nature, that in the end defy us. See his volume *Identité et Realité*, 1908, *passim.*

6. It is the more important to emphasize the point on which I have been insisting because in all recent discussion of the function of purely natural agencies there have entered considerations which were not present to the minds of the great thinkers who were dealing with the problem at the end of the eighteenth and the beginning of the nineteenth centuries. I mean the considerations suggested by the modern scientific doctrine of evolution. Darwin's theory was, indeed, an exclusively biological theory,—an attempt to explain how new species of plants and animals might be conceived as originating by a slow accumulation, under specific conditions, of minute advantageous variations from the type of pre-existing species. But, at the time of the publication of his epoch-making book in 1859, the idea of evolution was, so to speak, in the air; and Herbert Spencer was already engaged in working out a conception, in truth quite different from Darwin's,—different, namely, especially in this respect that, according to it, not merely are species of living organisms developing, but the universe in its entirety is subject to a process of development, from the relatively homogeneous to the relatively heterogeneous, from the relatively unstable to the relatively stable, from the relatively indefinite to the relatively definite. Now, the consideration which in this connexion I desire to press follows immediately from what I have already been urging. If by 'the universe in its entirety' be meant Reality as a whole, the totality of all that is, then from the very nature of the case there can be no 'evolution' of the universe, there can only be 'evolution' of constituents contained

within it. For the very conception of 'evolution' necessarily implies two things,—namely, something that as evolving is changing its character and an environment, which need not, indeed, be unchanging, but which must, at least, be relatively more stable than that which it encompasses. And the conception implies further that there is interrelation between these. If, then, either of these factors be absent, there can be no evolution. Without something having the capacity of changing there could be nothing to evolve; without an environment this 'something' would be an 'absolute becoming',—that is to say, merely blank inexplicable change. Clearly, therefore, Reality in its entirety, the totality of all that is, cannot, as such, be in a condition of evolution, because there can be no environment of Reality as a whole. In fact, we become at once involved in contradiction when we so much as talk of change itself on the part of Reality as a whole. For, whenever we speak of change, we are always assuming that there is a reason for such change, and moreover a reason for which we are justified in asking to be furnished. And the reason for any change can never be found in that change itself, but must be sought in something beyond it. Consequently, if the whole of *physical* reality be in a condition of movement or change, we are logically constrained to the admission that this whole of *physical* reality has a non-physical environment, and that this non-physical environment must be of such a character as to be capable of determining the direction along which the physical, as a whole, is changing.

It is just on this account that all philosophies based

on the conception of evolution as an ultimate principle, in contradistinction to a scientific theory of evolution, evince themselves as so eminently unsatisfactory, and wear the aspect almost of fairy tales. "Once upon a time" there was an initial concourse of atoms, "once upon a time" there was an unconscious will, "once upon a time" there was an undifferentiated Space-Time, or what not; and the story of evolution you may in some measure contrive to unfold, if only you are content to start with "once upon a time". But the true crux of the situation lies precisely there; and the philosophical problem is not so much as touched while that enigma is left standing.

7. If, then, the cosmological argument be interpreted as I have been trying to show it should be interpreted, the conclusion it entitles us to draw is that the realm of nature is not the whole of Reality, that the existence of nature being contingent existence is dependent upon a mode of Being that is not contingent but necessary. In itself, however, the argument throws no light upon the character of this absolutely necessary Being. It prepares the way for theism; but it does not, in itself, entitle us to assert that the self-explanatory ground of nature is a conscious Mind or Personality. And I do not think there is any purely speculative argument that will avail to establish that. We have got now to proceed empirically, by examining, namely, the various facts and aspects of nature, inclusive of man, that fall within the sphere of our observation, and by detecting, if we can, the indications they afford of the kind of reality upon which they depend. We have got, in

short, to survey this world of ours, so far as we can, impartially, without setting out with preconceived assumptions or weaving fanciful schemes of thought that may prove to be incompatible with the facts we discover.

THE TELEOLOGICAL ARGUMENT

1. I WILL begin this lecture by directing attention to a famous passage in Hume's *Enquiry*, with which every student of philosophy will be familiar. The passage runs thus: "All the objects of human reason or enquiry may naturally be divided into two kinds, to wit, *relations of ideas* and *matters of fact*. Of the first kind are the sciences of geometry, algebra, and arithmetic; and in short, every affirmation which is either intuitively or demonstratively certain. *That the square of the hypothenuse is equal to the square of the two sides* is a proposition which expresses a relation between these figures. *That three times five is equal to the half of thirty* expresses a relation between these numbers. Propositions of this kind are discoverable by the mere operation of thought, without dependence on what is anywhere existent in the universe. Though there never were a circle or triangle in nature, the truths demonstrated by Euclid would for ever retain their certainty and evidence. Matters of fact, which are the second objects of human reason, are not ascertained in the same manner; nor is our evidence

of their truth, however great, of a like nature with the foregoing. The contrary of every matter of fact is still possible; because it can never imply a contradiction, and is conceived by the mind with the same facility and distinctness as if ever so conformable to reality. *That the sun will not rise to-morrow* is no less intelligible a proposition, and implies no more contradiction, than the affirmation, *that it will rise.* We should in vain, therefore, attempt to demonstrate its falsehood. Were it demonstratively false, it would imply a contradiction, and could never be distinctly conceived by the mind."

In this passage, Hume was trying to make manifest the distinction between those truths which are *not* necessarily about *existent* realities and those truths, or what we ordinarily take to be truths, which *are* about existent realities. And he was pointing out, in his own way, that the kinds of relation which hold good in regard to the first class of truths are not identical with the kinds of relation which we find exemplified in the world of existent fact. Of the former are such relations as those of implication, as when we say that the assertion 'A is different from B' implies the assertion that 'B is different from A', of compatibility and incompatibility, of reason and consequent, and so on; of the latter are such relations as those of simultaneity, of succession, of substance and attribute, and above all, as Hume conceived, of cause and effect. What Hume was endeavouring to show was that there is a certainty attaching to the one class of propositions such as can never attach to those of the other class.

We are accustomed to find the evidence for the existence of any particular thing in the fact that we have observed it, or that others have observed it,— that is to say, such evidence is made to rest ultimately on the use of the senses. According to the familiar proverb, "seeing is believing". But, now, quite obviously we do not believe that $2 + 2 = 4$ because the evidence of our eyes is unimpeachable. On the contrary, we are face to face here with a sheer intellectual necessity, from which, eyes or no eyes, there is no way of escape. Our belief in this proposition is not provisional, not liable to modification in consequence of future discoveries; it is final and irrevocable. The proposition expresses, in other words, what has been called an *a priori* truth, a truth, that is, which is independent of experience, not in the sense that we could have become aware of it had we had no experience, but in the sense that there is no one specific fact of experience on which it rests, and no conceivable fact of experience which could upset or disprove it. Moreover, however useful mathematics may be as a *means* of determining the nature of existent facts, it has itself no direct contact with the realm of existence. Progress of knowledge in the domain of mathematical truth does not necessarily involve progress in our knowledge of nature. It helps no doubt indirectly to the increase of such knowledge by enlarging our capacity of obtaining accurate and reliable knowledge of the natural world. Because the very circumstance that mathematics is independent of experience, in the sense I have indicated, entails that there is not, and cannot be, any contradiction between mathematical truth and existent reality. Yet by mathematics we can never prove that anything exists, nor can any character which we are led to assign to existent entities ever influence, or in any way affect, the truths of mathematics. The two realms are, of course, related (if they were not, the scientist would find mathematics of no use to him), but the relation is of such a kind as to render the possibility of conflict out of the question. And what I have just been saying of mathematical truths holds likewise of the principles of formal logic. They too are *a priori*, they too are incontrovertible, for the simple reason that the thinker who tried to controvert them would, in doing so, be obliged to make use of them. Further, they are no less exempt from collision with our beliefs about existent realities than mathematical truths are; and, once more, like the truths of mathematics, they do not of themselves add anything to our knowledge of existent realities.

When, now, we come to knowledge of what Hume called 'matters of fact', there can be no such *infallible* certainty as that which we have just seen attaches to the *a priori* truths of mathematics and of formal logic. In the long run, as I have said, what we know, or suppose ourselves to know, of existent reality rests upon perceptual observation. And for two reasons, such observation, even of the most careful and circumspect kind, is always exposed to the possibility of error. On the one hand, the act of observing, or of perceiving, is, as we have seen, an excessively complicated act, involving not only the facility of discriminating the features of the object presented, but also the bringing to bear of a number of acquired notions or concepts, by the help of which we interpret the object immediately before us. On the other hand, every object or event in nature is enormously complex; and it is never possible for an observing mind to become aware of all the elements or characteristics of which the object or event consists. In observing the facts of nature, we are, therefore, perpetually liable to misinterpret those facts, either on account of overlooking what *is* there to be observed, or on account of illegitimately reading into them what is *not* there to be observed.[1] Not only so. In scientific procedure, doubtless, a strenuous effort is made to minimize, as far as possible, these defects of ordinary observation by exercising deliberate and judiciously devised control over the process in question, and by a more careful and relevant employment of already acquired knowledge. Furthermore, starting from direct observation of certain particular things and events, the scientist endeavours to extend his view both in space and in time, and to afford justification for believing in the existence of numerous particular things and events, such as planets and stars and ice-ages, which are either wholly or partially beyond the reach of direct observation. Yet that is not the main function of science. Its main function is, as I have previously pointed out, to reach those general principles which are called laws of nature, —expressions, namely, of the constant manner in

[1] "Those who have never tried to observe accurately will be surprised to find how difficult a business it is. There is not one person in a hundred who can describe the commonest occurrence with even an approach to accuracy."—T. H. Huxley, *Introductory Science Primer*, pp. 16–17.

which particular facts or parts of existent reality are related to one another, or of the constant order in which certain types of natural events take place. In other words, the fundamental aim of science is to attain a systematic body of timeless truths about the various sorts or classes of temporal things,—truths which, being timeless and general, can be applied, at any time or place, to justify assertions respecting so-called matters of fact. What, however, I am concerned at present especially to emphasize respecting these general truths or laws of nature is this, that, however highly probable they may be,—and a large number of them are so highly probable that no competent person entertains the slightest doubt in regard to them— yet no one of them is either self-evident or can be *absolutely* proved or demonstrated, as is the case with mathematical truths. All the inductive arguments of science thus lead only to conclusions, or statements of empirical laws, which are more or less probable. And even their probability depends upon a certain assumption in regard to the realm of existence, which assumption again can never be unquestionably and decisively justified. This ultimate assumption has been variously formulated. Mill described it as the principle of the uniformity of nature, or of universal causation; and Huxley as the principle that nothing happens by chance, that there are in nature no real accidents, in the sense of events which have no cause. More recently, it has been described as the assumption that throughout nature there are comparatively few kinds of permanent substances, that the changes of these are all subject to laws, and that the variety of nature is due to the

varying combinations of these few elementary substances. But the important point to notice here is that,
however the assumption be formulated, it is, and must
remain, *an assumption*,—an assumption which is
neither self-evident nor susceptible of strict demon-
stration, either on grounds of experience or by logical
reasoning. The most we can say is that it is an
assumption which is requisite if we are to attach any
considerable degree of probability to generalizations
with regard to the existent world.

There is, moreover, another limitation of science
of which it will be well to take note. Science is, as I
have said, primarily concerned to bring to light
general truths regarding the elements of which things
are composed and the general laws which in their
modes of behaviour they exemplify. Consequently,
it is well-nigh exclusively concerned with the repeatable
features of the world of existence, and all the main
propositions of science are about these. But, in point
of fact, nature, according to a well-known maxim,
never *exactly* repeats itself. Each single existent thing,
while, so far as its general characters are concerned,
conforming to some specific type, is, as a whole,
differentiated in a subtle and indefinable way from
other instances of its kind; each is, in short, a unique
individual. Yet to this individuality as such science
pays no heed; its business is with types and sub-types
and with cases of deviation from these; and, in dealing
with a complex totality, the ordinary scientific procedure is to break it up into its simpler constituents.
As a recent writer has put it: "Botany knows no
flower, Zoology no animal; they know only the laws

of certain functions and processes of which these terms represent the familiar theatre."[1]

2. Now, the central affirmation of the religious consciousness finds, we shall agree, expression in the proposition 'God conceived as the Divine Mind exists'. This proposition purports to be the assertion of what Hume would have called 'a matter of fact', —that is to say, it is not a proposition of the self-evident, absolutely indubitable character of mathematical propositions or the principles of formal logic. But it is the assertion of a 'matter of fact' of an altogether unique and remarkable kind. I have just been saying that ultimately the evidence we appeal to in affirming the existence of any 'matter of fact' in the world around us is that afforded by perceptual experience. Yet obviously that criterion will not avail us here. "No man hath seen God at any time." Or, in the words of the old Greek philosopher, Empedocles, "it is not possible for us to set God before our eyes, or to lay hold of him with our hands, which is the broadest way of persuasion that leads into the heart of man".

It is true that religious persons have more often than not refused to acquiesce in this dictum of Empedocles. The widespread notion of the occurrence of miracles, regarded as exceptional events affording direct perceptual evidence of God's existence, indicates how tenacious a hold the popular saying that 'seeing is believing' has continued to exert on the minds of men. Nevertheless, as T. H. Green once observed, "if faith were really belief in the occurrence of certain

[1] J. L. Stocks, *On the Nature and Grounds of Religious Belief*, p. 28.

miraculous events upon transmitted evidence of the senses of other people, its certainty would after all be merely a weaker form of the certainty of sense",[1] which is, in truth, no certainty at all.

If, then, we relinquish the endeavour to demonstrate the existence of God on purely *a priori* grounds, and if we likewise abandon the belief that such existence has been disclosed once for all through the medium of a miraculous revelation, can we discern by inspection of the facts of nature any evidence that will justify us in adhering still to the conviction which has been the inspiration of many of earth's noblest souls? I am going to show why I think we can. But it is not now, I hope, necessary to warn you against expecting, along these lines, any absolutely irrefragable proof of the central affirmation of the religious consciousness. Unique and *sui generis* though the belief we are concerned with is, yet still, even if that belief be justified, it is with a 'matter of fact' we have to do; and, as we have seen, in regard to *all* 'matters of fact', it is only a high degree of probability we can reach, never that indubitable certainty which is attainable in mathematics and in formal logic. Nor need that consideration in the least disconcert us. When we reflect upon the vast number of beliefs about 'matters of fact' which, although they can never be conclusively demonstrated, no sane person really for one moment supposes to be dubious, the circumstance to which I am alluding ought to occasion no misgiving. We have got, then, to proceed empirically; or, if you will, inductively; and by examining the various features and aspects of our portion of the cosmic whole, to try to fathom the indications they afford of the kind of reality that lies beyond. And if, in so doing, we reach a result to which attaches the degree of probability that belongs to the stable generalizations of science we may surely rest content.

In the *Phaedo*, Plato represents Socrates as chiding the physicists of his day for undertaking to explain all the phenomena of nature in purely mechanical fashion. They would even account for his presence there in prison, awaiting death, after he had been proffered and had rejected a means of escape, by giving an analysis of the material constituents of his bodily structure, completely ignoring that which was really the vital and significant fact in the whole situation,—the existence, namely, of his mind, and in particular of his mental capacity of judging and determining what was right and good. It was their exclusion of thought and intellect from having had any share in the sequence of events that seemed to Socrates so perverse; and, in this connexion, he was led to record the deep impression made upon him as a young man when he happened once to hear someone quoting a passage from a book of Anaxagoras to the effect that 'Mind (νοῦς) set all things in order' and 'had knowledge about everything'. Unhappily, he had to confess that when afterwards he procured the book and read it for himself his hopes were shattered; for, in the long run, Anaxagoras deserted his own principle and had recourse only to just those agencies on which the others had laid stress.

And, at the beginning of the *Metaphysics*, where

he was reviewing the work of his predecessors, Aristotle too laid stress on the same point. He insisted there that earth and air, fire and water, the elementary substances of which all bodies were taken by him to be composed, whatever else they might account for, obviously did not account for the fact that things manifest order and rightness, arrangement and beauty, and these surely called for recognition and explanation. So that when one man came forward and said that Mind is concerned in all this, determining the order and plan of the world, he seemed like a man in his sober senses in contrast with those who had spoken in the idle way referred to. Aristotle was, of course, alluding here to Anaxagoras, although later he had to acknowledge that Plato's judgment on the book of Anaxagoras as a whole was well founded. Anaxagoras had, in fact, merely caught a fleeting glimpse of what Plato and Aristotle were afterwards to work out more elaborately. They were persuaded that the ruling and directive function of Mind in the universe had got to be recognized, if an intelligible outlook on nature and human life was to be attained; otherwise, the whole course of things would have to be ascribed to the play of mere chance or accident. Foresight, intention, purpose,—these alone could exclude chance, and these appertained only to Mind.

3. The teleological argument, that is based on the admitted fact of order in the world which is taken to be indicative of purpose or design on the part of an ultimate Intelligence, dates back, then, to the early days of Greek reflexion. But I must confine attention here to considerations that may be advanced in its

support from the point of view of recent philosophical inquiry.

One all-important consideration which I would emphasize at the outset is this. The more thoroughly acquainted we become with the facts and ways of nature, the more strongly is there borne in upon us the conviction to which Kant gave expression in the concluding sections of the *Critique of Pure Reason*,— the conviction, namely, of the striking *adaptation* of nature to human thought and reason. In its very essence nature would seem to be intimately related to mind or intelligence. It is, at least, conceivable that it might have been quite otherwise, that nature might have been a mere chaos, in which similar events never occurred, in which universals had no exemplifications, relations no fixity, and the principles of logic no application. Now, in a 'nature' of that sort no rational mind could live; thought would find nothing to grasp; and, without something to think about, a thinking mind would be an impossibility. And thus we seem driven to conclude that there must be a correlation of the intellect and the intelligible in order that there can be either a rational human mind or knowledge, on its part, of nature.[1] As Kant put it, the principle of Intelligibility is the principle of the teleological judgment. We cannot avoid "regarding everything that can belong to the context of possible experience as if this experience formed an absolute but at the same time completely dependent and sensibly conditioned unity, and yet also at the same time as if the sum of all phenomena had a single

[1] *Cf. supra*, p. 71 *sqq.*

highest and all-sufficient ground beyond itself, namely a self-subsistent, original, creative reason."[1] Philip Wicksteed has left on record how recognition of the fact that the mathematical relations which the astronomer detects in the arrangement of material entities in space are identical with the mathematical relations with which the mathematician becomes acquainted in the quiet of his study had given a new meaning for him to the word that "man is the child of God", and had taught him to think of the rational intellect as reflecting far more explicitly than the senses ever can do the inner meaning and constitution of the universe.[2] And at the present day we find Sir James Jeans asserting practically the same thing. "Nature", he tells us, "seems very conversant with the rules of pure mathematics, as our mathematicians have formulated them, without drawing to any appreciable extent on their experience of the outer world"; and, in words I have already quoted, he avers that "the great architect of the universe now begins to appear as a pure mathematician".[3] Does not, then, this basal consideration of the intelligibility of nature, and of its consequent adaptation to the intellectual procedure of our minds, seem of itself to involve, as Sir James Jeans insists it does, that nature exhibits methods due to intelligence, that it is the medium or vehicle of thoughts which the human intellect can contemplate as though they were its own?

I am by no means oblivious of an objection, not without weight, that might be brought against the

[1] *Kritik der reinen Vernunft*, A, 672; B, 700.

[2] *The Reactions between Religion and Dogma*, 1920, p. 446.

[3] *The Mysterious Universe*, p. 130 *sqq.*

conclusion thus suggested. You have not, it may be contended, excluded the possibility of another explanation. If it be assumed that the finite mind is itself a product of nature, it would not be surprising that the ways in which that mind comes to think should correspond with the ways in which nature's operations are carried on, or that the basis of all logical necessity should be the necessity of fact. You forget, it may be urged, that the human mind is not an abstraction, that it lives and thinks only in and through its concrete experience, and that what we are inclined to ascribe to it as its unique achievements might rather be said to be what goes to its very making as the outcome of nature. Yes; but he who argues thus has departed so widely from the merely mechanical conception of 'nature' that it may fairly be questioned whether he is not really conceding what he is wishful to deny. In a somewhat similar manner, Tyndall maintained, in the celebrated Belfast Address of 1874, that if we "radically change our notions of 'matter' " we may discern in matter "the promise and potency of all terrestrial life". But, as Dr. Martineau pointed out immediately afterwards, the 'change' virtually meant that there was being imported into 'matter' just precisely what was required to be got out of it, and that, therefore, there was no wonder if from it all things might be derived. "Such extremely clever Matter,—matter that is up to everything, even to writing *Hamlet*, and finding out its own evolution, may fairly be regarded as a little too modest in its disclaimer of the attributes of Mind."[1]

[1] *Essays, Reviews and Addresses*, vol. iv, 1891, p. 175.

4. The teleological argument, or the argument from or to design, may be, and often has been, crudely stated; and when it is so stated it is certainly exposed to criticism of a sufficiently damaging kind. But it can be presented in a form that is not crude, and as thus presented it is not to be so lightly set aside as many writers have supposed. Without attempting to survey the whole field, I will draw attention to two sets of facts that are of singular impressiveness,— on the one hand, the adaptation of inorganic nature to life, and more especially to the life of man; and, on the other hand, the peculiarities of living organisms as such.

(a) It is unquestionable that the conditions of inorganic nature on this planet, at least, are extraordinarily well adapted to the requirements of living organisms in their nurture and growth. Quite recently, a distinguished American biologist, Professor Lawrence J. Henderson, has been insisting that, if the physico-chemical system be regarded, not in abstraction by itself, but in its bearing on the life of the organisms, the manifold forms of which it determines and renders possible, it becomes surprisingly apparent that the fundamental properties of the three chemical elements —carbon, hydrogen and oxygen—and of certain of their compounds—water and carbonic acid—as also the wide distribution of these elements and compounds —exhibit a *maximum* of fitness for the needs of precisely such living creatures as we actually find upon this earth. Countless other distributions, countless other conjunctions of properties, would have been no bit less antecedently possible; and yet we find in nature just *that* distribution, just *that* conjunction of properties, which is *fittest* for the maintenance of life. Not only so. Each and all of these many unique properties of the three elements are favourable to the process of evolution and the connexion between them, infinitely improbable as the result of chance,[1] is in truth only fully intelligible, even when mechanistically explained, as a *preparation* for the evolutionary process. Since, then, it is incredible that all this amazing adaptation, all this extraordinary preparation for what was to be, could come about through the play of merely mechanical processes, Proféssor Henderson concludes that it is ultimately due to the working of an intelligent mind of far-reaching discernment and foresight.

Several objections have, indeed, been brought against this reasoning. It has been maintained, for instance, that the fulfilment of the conditions referred to seem really to be very local and temporary; that in all likelihood they are not fulfilled now in the greater part of the universe, that they were certainly not fulfilled in former ages on the earth itself, and that almost certainly they will cease to be fulfilled on the earth itself in the distant future. Consequently, so it has been contended, "it is not antecedently improbable that even very peculiar conditions should be fulfilled for a comparatively small region of a universe which is indefinitely extended in space and time". But none of these objections seem to me either strong or convincing. I cannot see, for instance, what the fact, if it be a fact, that the number of inhabited worlds in

---

[1] *Cf.* Franz Brentano, *Vom Dasein Gottes*, 1929, p. 357 *sqq.* Brentano shows in detail how infinitely improbable it is, according to the Calculus of Probability, that the apparent teleology in nature is due to accidental collocations and dispositions of the elements.

space is comparatively small, has to do with the question. That there should be no adaptation to living organisms in those portions of the universe where there are none is scarcely an indication of thoughtless negligence. The objection would only be of weight if it were possible to point to a world on which there are living beings but where there is no such adaptation. Furthermore, if there be the adaptation, which admittedly there now is, of the environment to life on this planet, then clearly it must have been prepared for in the long geological ages which have preceded this, and during the still more remote astronomical periods of the formation of the solar system. In short, you cannot cut out our tiny portion of the universe as a definitely isolated section or region. On the contrary, it has ramifications which extend indefinitely far; and, if the adaptation we are considering subsists here and now, it is certain that its conditions cannot be confined to what is "very local and temporary", but must have extended over a vastly wide range, both in space and time.[1] To say that these peculiarly teleological aspects of nature are after all but the result of the infinite castings of the cosmic dice (to use Trendelenberg's illustration) is, therefore, very like asserting that the *Iliad* or *Hamlet* may be supposed to be a collocation of letters, accidentally arrived at

[1] It is for this reason that I think we are entitled to reject Mill's contention (*Logic*, Bk. iii, ch. xxi, § 4) that in distant parts of the stellar regions, where the phenomena may be entirely unlike those with which we are acquainted, the law of causation may not hold. If there were any part of the material universe not subject to the law in question, it could not be without influence upon that portion within the range of our observation, and would thus render a universal relation of cause and effect in the latter more than precarious.

in the course of infinite shufflings of the alphabetic symbols.

(*b*) Turn, now, to the organisms themselves. Admittedly an organism is a complex system of an extremely intricate kind, consisting of an assembly of delicately adjusted cell-mechanisms, working co-ordinately in the most unerring manner, a system which is remarkably well adapted to preserve itself in the presence of varying conditions. An organism is a self-conserving system, building itself up by appropriating from its environment suitable material, which it transforms into its own tissue; responding continuously to changes in its surroundings by adaptive processes; and, finally, regulating in the minutest fashion the action of each of its parts in the interest of the whole.[1] Now, so long as organisms were believed to have originated in their present forms, and with all their specialized organs 'ready made', the notion that the adaptation of part to whole, of whole to environment, of organ to function, implied special design in each individual case seemed not only plausible but well-nigh inevitable. But a view of that sort was at once seen to be untenable when it became evident that every organic structure has come to be what it now is as a result of a long series of successive and gradual modifications. Yet the theory of evolution has been driving those who have penetrated most profoundly into its meaning to a conception of 'design' on a far larger scale than any which was contemplated by Paley. If we survey the course which evolution has

[1] Consider, for instance, the network of intricate bodily processes that take place on the occasion of so ordinary a performance as lifting the arm.

taken in our comparatively small region of the cosmos, it becomes apparent that it has been in a significant direction. Through a line of species which have had to adapt themselves to their environment, it has led to the emergence of an intelligent and rational being, who *adapts* his environment to himself, who largely *makes*, so to speak, his own environment and is not wholly made by it. It would seem, then, well-nigh impossible for a reflective mind to look upon this terminus of the process as a mere by-product, as a mere accident of evolution; or, indeed, as anything else than the 'end' which has been all along determining the course of development. 'Nature', one might almost venture to assert, really does exhibit a 'trend' or 'bias' to the advent of intelligence. In short, whether we have regard to the structure and functioning of individual organisms, or whether we have regard to the evolutionary process generally, we appear to be driven to the conclusion that in the organic world there is a teleological or purposive principle at work, directing and modifying what would otherwise be mechanically determined elements.

5. It was, I take it, some such conviction as this that led Professor A. N. Whitehead, in his volume of Gifford Lectures on *Process and Reality*, to carry the notion of 'organism' right down the scale of physical existence. An atom of hydrogen, with its electron dancing round the central nucleus, is, he maintains, an 'organism'; it is no mere inert particle, but exhibits a particular 'pattern' as grasped in the unity of a real event. In a molecule of water, the electron of the hydrogen atom still dances round its nucleus; but it

does so now in accordance with the general *organic plan* of the molecule as a whole, and no longer as it did when in the free state. And so, in like manner, ascending the hierarchy of being, the concrete enduring entities are, he insists, everywhere 'organisms', in each of which the 'plan' of the *whole* influences the characters of the various subordinate 'organisms' which enter into it. Thus, for example, an electron within a living body is a totally different thing from an electron outside of it, and is so by reason of the 'plan' of the body. But such principle of modification is perfectly general throughout nature, and represents no property peculiar to living things alone.

It is a daring conception, this, of one of the most original philosophic thinkers of the present time, who discerns with clear insight the drift of modern scientific theorizing. Does it in any way undermine the idea of design in nature? If you vastly extend the range of what, at all events, looks like purposive activity, if you find even the constituents of so-called inert matter manifesting signs of intelligible 'plan', do you thereby lessen the force of the evidence tending to show the existence of a supreme and guiding intelligence? Professor Whitehead, at any rate, will not have it so. He finds it essential to postulate the being of God in order even to account for the selection of those 'plans' which the organisms of nature follow and as the ground of the rationality which they exemplify. Nature herself we may suppose, he suggests, if we allow ourselves to use the misleading personification at all, to be like a sleep-walker who executes trains of purposive acts without knowing that he does so. Yet the 'plan' itself cannot have originated without a wakeful and alert intelligence. Let 'nature' be as unconscious as you please, the stronger is the suggestion that the marvellous 'adaptations' which pervade 'nature' must be the deliberate designs of One who neither slumbers nor sleeps.

6. So, too, the analogy which was formerly drawn between artificial machines and living organisms we can now see to have been a false analogy. Life or vitality, as the biologists of the present day conceive it, is a property *sui generis*, which cannot even in theory be traced to the physical and chemical properties of the complex in which it appears. The living organic structure, without ceasing to be physico-chemical, has acquired quite new intrinsic properties, and quite new extrinsic properties in relation to other structures —qualities and properties which only spring into being when the particular complex which we call a vital organism dawns upon the scene. The scientist of to-day applies this notion of 'emergence', as it has been named, not only to vital phenomena but to all stages of increasing complexity in nature. There is 'emergence' of new qualities, he holds, at every substantial complication of the structural 'plan',— from the electron to the atom, from the atom to the molecule, from the molecule to the crystal, and so on, until we reach the living organism. For instance, from what we know of oxygen itself and of hydrogen itself, it would be impossible to deduce or to predict the properties of water, in which these two gases are combined together in definite proportions. The properties that result are novelties—they are emer-

gently new. Accepting, then, this 'emergence' theory with regard to living things, is there justification for the view, which some philosophers have sanctioned, that it being granted there is no longer need for the hypothesis of a directing Mind, so far as the peculiarities of living organisms are concerned? The coming into being of 'emergent' qualities is surely not to be regarded as a mere freak on the part of nature. On the contrary, does it not indicate with sufficient clearness the presence of features in the material world that become simply enigmatical and unintelligible if they are to be taken as so much 'brute' fact? They are not self-explanatory, any more than are the causal events which we were considering in the last lecture. They must have a ground or source, and they seem irresistibly to point to an immanent teleology, which can only be traceable to a conscious Mind or Soul. Not only so. If the 'emergence' theory be on the right lines, there would seem to be disclosed throughout nature the presence of what Lloyd Morgan described as a 'directive activity', of which 'the manner of going on in all natural events', as he called it, is the embodiment. Now, such a directive activity cannot itself be an emergent term in the series. The whole evolutionary plan, with what has been named its upward *nisus*, would appear to be the manifestation of a single and indivisible spiritual agency.

A perplexing question confronts us at the end of these reflexions concerning which I must be brief. Does the theory of emergent evolution get over the difficulty that beset the older evolutionary theories, and enable us to offer an intelligible account of the way in which minds or souls may be regarded as coming into existence?

We may be here reminded of an ancient theological controversy. On the one hand, Tertullian maintained in his book, entitled *De Anima*, that souls are generated from other souls in a similar manner and at the same time as their bodies are generated from other bodies. On the other hand, Pelagius and his followers, who advocated the doctrine of free will in opposition to that of total depravity, taunted the upholders of the dogma of original sin with holding Tertullian's views, which they christened traducian (*tradux*, a transfer or passing over). Accordingly, the name 'traducianism' was given to Tertullian's theory that souls are generated from other souls, whereas the theory that souls are created directly by God was called 'creationism'.

7. I do not, of course, propose to enter here into the merits of that controversy. But it will be of interest to note the tendency on the part of many modern psychologists to favour the creationist view as against traducianism. Lotze, for example rejected as utterly unthinkable the notion that the organic body, in the process of being formed, educes the soul from itself; nor did he conceive it possible that the soul of the child could be 'split off', so to speak, from the soul of the parent. Consequently, we are, it seemed to him, forced to the 'dim conjecture' that the supreme Mind, on the occasion of the quietly advancing formation of the organic germ, produces out of itself the soul appropriate to the growing organism. And James Ward, although he considered that the creationist theory exceeds the limits of scientific inquiry, was yet

of opinion that it, at least, involves no contradiction and is consistent, as the traducian theory is not, with the two cardinal principles of psychology,—the individuality of the conscious subject and the duality of subject and object in the conscious subject's experience.[1]

It is worth while asking, in the present connexion, why psychologists of such eminence have felt thus constrained, from the point of view of their science, to express their preference for the creationist hypothesis. I think it was not only because they recognized the sheer impossibility of conceiving how the mental life could have been formed from what is purely physical, but also because they realized the tremendous difficulties of the only other hypothesis, short of that which we are considering, the hypothesis, namely, that an individual mind comes, in some way, to be generated by the minds of the parents. This latter conception is based on a crude analogy with what happens in the case of the bodily organism; but, in truth, the supposed analogy breaks down. Between the bodily organism of the parent and that of the offspring there is a continuity of an unmistakable kind. But there is no such continuity between the *mind* of the parent and the *mind* of the child. The child's mind was never, at any stage of its development, a part of the mind of its parent or parents. No doubt, certain mental traits of the parents may, in a sense, be said to be 'inherited' by the child, yet not in the sense in which bodily traits are said to be inherited. What is

[1] *Cf.* Lotze, *Medicinische Psychologie*, p. 164 *sqq.*; *Microcosmus*, Eng. trans., vol. i, p. 390 *sqq.*; James Ward, *Psychological Principles*, p. 423 *sqq.*

'heritable' so far as the mental life is concerned, is not, so Dr. Ward used to contend, individuality or character, but simply a tendency on the part of the new individual to develop certain ancestral characteristics. Consequently, although the 'origin of a soul' is altogether beyond our ken, it seemed to Dr. Ward that the conception of a supreme Mind from whom finite minds emanate does provide a rational explanation of what would otherwise remain a baffling enigma. He admitted, of course, that the term 'creation' is, in this context, altogether inappropriate; a soul is certainly not a 'manufactured article' in the sense in which Clerk Maxwell conceived an atom to be. It is just here, however, that the theory of 'emergent evolution', in some such form as Lloyd Morgan has presented, comes to our aid. If, not only at the level of life or of mind, but everywhere and everywhen throughout nature, there is manifested a directive Source or purposive Activity (understanding, that is, by 'Activity' not physical energy but mental activity), then it is not inconceivable that in some way which we, indeed, can only dimly fathom,[1] finite minds should emanate from a Mind that is supreme.

8. Looking back, then, on the path we have been traversing in this lecture, I think we may conclude that the confident assertion so often made that there is no inductive argument which tends in the least to render the existence of a personal Deity so much as probable is devoid of justification. The term 'personal', when so employed, has, it is true, its dangers, against

[1] "Not to know how a thing can be", F. H. Bradley once observed, "is no disproof that the thing must be so and is."

which it behoves us to be on our guard. It may lead to a crude anthropomorphism which the slightest reflexion ought to be sufficient to dispel. What, however, we want the term 'personality', in this context, to express is that, so far from being identical with the 'Absolute' or the whole of Reality, the Divine Being is an individual, living, self-conscious Mind. The nature of that Mind may—must, indeed—indefinitely transcend the potentialities of human personalities, and embrace capacities as far removed from our apprehension as our science is beyond the range of animal perception, but whatever else it may contain, its essential characteristics cannot be other than those of rational intelligence, thought and volition. But to this consideration I shall return in the lectures which follow.

VALUES AND THE MORAL ARGUMENT

I WAS trying in the last lecture to bring into clear relief those aspects of nature which seem to indicate a reality other than and transcending nature, and which also lead us to form some conception, imperfect though it be, of the kind of reality which is thus indicated. I directed attention, first of all, to the significant manner in which the realm of physical nature is adapted to human thought and reason. Turn where you will, the course of nature seems to be intelligible and to exemplify principles which human intelligence itself employs in reaching truth and acquiring knowledge. Thus nature would appear to be the expression or manifestation of thoughts which we can intellectually grasp and understand. I went on to notice the striking adaptation of physical nature, in our corner of the universe, at least, to the needs and requirements of living organisms,—an adaptation so intricate and so far-reaching as to render well-nigh incredible the notion that it has come about through the play of merely mechanical processes. I turned, then, to consider the structure of these living organisms themselves, and pointed to the surprising correlation of the most delicately adjusted factors, which it is simply impossible to account for as a fortuitous arrangement of material elements. We are, in fact, constrained to recognize that every part of an organism must be regarded as actually or potentially acting on and being acted on by the other parts (and by the environment), so as to form with them a self-conserving system. In other words, in describing even the most rudimentary of living organisms, we are compelled to have resort to teleological terminology, and to think of them as exhibiting intention and purpose.

But, then, so soon as we have reached that result the question is at once forced upon us whether in using such words as 'function', 'purpose', 'means' and 'end', in describing the operations of living organisms themselves, we have not virtually been looking upon these organisms not as acted upon by merely mechanical environment, but as in teleological connexion with that which while other than they is yet in truth not radically independent of them. Have we not, that is to say, discarded the notion of mechanism altogether, and implicitly acknowledged that a teleological principle is really involved in the processes which we have been accustomed to look upon as purely mechanical? I tried to show reason for answering this question in the affirmative. Roughly speaking, the scientist is now confronted at various stages in physical investigation with facts which indicate the presence of inherent co-ordination at the basis of what was formerly conceived to be capable of being interpreted mechanically. Recent discoveries in physics and chemistry have radically modified our outlook on nature. The Newtonian conception of matter, as consisting ultimately of inert, impenetrable atoms, has been tacitly relinquished. On the one hand, an atom is now seen to be what may not inappropriately be called an organic structure, in which mass, form and internal activities are co-ordinated in a manner which is not only specific but is maintained. "An atom", as Professor J. S. Haldane has expressed it, "tends to maintain intense co-ordinated internal specific activity, which does not become dissipated in its environment, and on which both its mass and its other properties depend." Now, of all this no account can be furnished in terms of the Newtonian physics. And, on the other hand, the activity of an atom is connected in a close and intricate way with its environment, so that its absorption and emission of electro-magnetic waves would seem to be analogous to the reaction between a living organism and its environment. In short, throughout the realm of physical nature clear indications appear to be afforded of a purposiveness more or less akin to that exhibited by living beings.

Furthermore, I endeavoured to show that the real significance of the fact of evolution is very far from being what has frequently been supposed. It is true that Darwin held that the argument from design in nature fails in view of the law of natural selection, but he was thinking of design in the crude form in which it had been presented by Paley. And, as embodied in the writings, for instance, of Herbert Spencer, the theory of evolution implied that the organic proceeded originally from what was in the strict sense inorganic.

But we saw that, evolution or no evolution, most biologists of the present day would dismiss that notion as a sheer incongruity. For them, therefore, evolution takes on a very different significance. In tracing life back and back to its primordial beginnings, they are not seeking to derive its origin from 'inorganic matter', in the old sense of that term; they are seeking rather to transform the idea of the 'inorganic', and to discern even in the 'matter' of the physicist organization, system, selective activity. The most determined and thoroughgoing attempt hitherto made to work out this view is, as I indicated, that of Dr. Whitehead. "The concrete enduring entities are", he writes, "organisms, so that the plan of the *whole* influences the very characters of the various subordinate organisms which enter into it. In the case of an animal, the mental states enter into the plan of the total organism and thus modify the plans of the successive subordinate organisms until the ultimate smallest organisms, such as electrons, are reached. Thus an electron within a living body is different from an electron outside it, by reason of the plan of the body. The electron blindly runs either within or without the body; but it runs within the body in accordance with its character within the body; that is to say, in accordance with the general plan of the body, and this plan includes the mental state. But this principle of modification is perfectly general throughout nature, and represents no property peculiar to living bodies."[1] To put the case briefly, we have to conceive, as I have said, not only of a vast hierarchy of subordinate patterns, but in the

[1] *Science and the Modern World*, pp. 111–112.

long run of one pervasive "pattern of patterns", of one coherent "pattern", as constituting the course of nature, far as we may be from being able to formulate the scheme of this "pattern". Thus, then, we are brought once more to see that purposiveness, adaptation, design, does not spring from that which to start with is fortuitous, but is at the very heart of the processes of nature.

So much, at present, concerning our natural environment. But, as we have repeatedly had occasion to note, there is for rational minds not only a natural but also a spiritual environment. Not, indeed, that these two are in any opposition or are violently separated from one another. If what I have just been urging be not altogether groundless, obviously we cannot differentiate the natural from the spiritual as the mechanical from the non-mechanical. The two must be, in fact, constantly interwoven in the world of our experience. None the less, the natural and the spiritual may be essentially distinguishable, and be susceptible of different treatment. There are in our environment, namely, not only actually existent entities and events but ideals calling to be 'realized', values, as it is now customary to call them; and in our human lives the experience or consciousness of value is no less fundamental than the experience or consciousness of things and events. A human mind is not only perceptive, it is likewise appreciative; its intellectual activity involves at every turn appreciation of worth or value as well as consciousness of objects in space and time. It is, then, this spiritual environment I wish now more explicitly to consider; but, in order that I may profitably do so, I must be allowed first of all to dwell upon a philosophical distinction which is, in this connexion, of first-rate importance.

1. The distinction to which I refer is that between "being" or "reality" and "existence". To state the case as briefly as possible, the term 'being' or 'reality' is a very much wider and more comprehensive term than the term 'existence'. There is a great deal that is 'real' or 'has being' that cannot rightly be said to exist. 'Existence' appertains, in fact, only to individuals, whereas universals, qualities, relations, truths, although 'real', do not, as such, 'exist'. The blue sky is, for instance, an existent; but the quality 'blue' is not by itself an existent. The specific blue of the sky is a feature or characteristic of an existent thing; but if it is regarded in abstraction from that which it thus characterizes it is a universal, a universal which characterizes numerous things. Now, it is an elementary principle in logic that ultimate terms, such as this term 'existence', are indefinable. But, although we cannot define the term 'existence', we can furnish a criterion by means of which it may be recognized. We ought, namely, to speak of entities as existing only when they are in time,—that is to say, when we can point to some time *at* which they are (not excluding, of course, the possibility of their existing at all times). Indeed, I am inclined to think we can go further. It seems to be a fact that everything which is in time is, in some form or another, active. Certainly, it *is* true that everything which is active is an existent; and if the converse be true, that every existent implies or involves activity, we should have, at once, a ready

means of distinguishing an existent from what is not an existent.

In a sense, this distinction between 'being' and 'existence' was implicitly drawn by Plato. What he called 'forms' or 'essences' (ἰδέαι or εἴδη),—beauty, goodness, justice, etc.,—he certainly conceived to have 'being', and 'being' of a supreme kind; but he did not regard them as existents, in our sense of the term; they were not, that is to say, temporal entities, such as those we encounter in the realm of sense-experience. In recent times, however, the distinction in question has been forced to the front largely by the labours of several noted mathematicians. More particularly, Bolzano and Frege, in the middle of the last century, saw quite clearly that if mathematics were concerned merely with mental entities—with so-called 'ideas' or 'concepts',[1] namely,—the science of mathematics could not possess the certitude or exactness which is claimed for it. The laws of logic,—such a law as that, for example, of non-contradiction,—on which its whole structure depends, would be on a level with the so-called laws of association in psychology; and mathematical truth would resolve itself into an outcome of human caprice or imagination. They were driven, therefore, to the conclusion that, in judging and inferring, what-I-judge and what-I-infer must be both other than and independent of the mental acts involved in such judging or inferring. There must be, that is to say, truths, as real entities,—truths which are true whether anyone thinks them or no.

[1] As, for instance, Hume held what he called 'relations of ideas' to be. *Cf. supra*, p. 190 *sqq.*

These entities do not, of course, *exist*; they are not, that is to say, in time. They are not members of the world of physical things and events, nor yet of the world of mental beings and events. Yet they are not outcasts or wayfarers; for the old Cartesian division of reality into mind and matter is far from being exhaustive. In addition, there is, at least, a realm in which truths, universals, numbers, relations, etc., have their being. These entities *are*; and, as they do not exist, they may be said to *subsist* (*zu bestehen*, or to hold good).

Furthermore, it is generally allowed that our judgments are either true or false. Yet the moment we are in earnest with such statements, we are compelled to admit that if my judgment that $2 + 2 = 4$ is true, then it *is* true that $2 + 2 = 4$, whether I happen to think it or no. Such a truth is not made true, that is to say, by being believed. So that it seems self-evident that if it is true that $2 + 2 = 4$, then that proposition always will be true and always has been true. Truths are eternal, in Spinoza's sense of the word, that is to say, they are timeless, whereas beliefs belong to the biographies of persons and, as such, are necessarily dated or temporal in character. And, more recently, philosophic thinkers so distinguished as Meinong and Husserl have strenuously insisted that only if there are such entities as subsistents can there be a science of logic at all. Pure Logic, they point out, is admittedly the science of the *forms* of something (*etwas*), that is to say, of the general characteristics of something. But the entities which have these forms are not physical substances or events, nor yet mental substances or events. A stone wall does not *contradict* a wind; nor is a state of mind a conclusion of a syllogism. In short, there are, at least, two main kinds of being, the existing and the subsisting. It is only what Meinong called our "prejudice in favour of the actual" which induces us to ignore or repudiate the latter of these. To sum up, then, these entities do not *exist*, but they *are* in another way; and their mode of being may be called that of *subsistence*. And of such subsistent entities several kinds may be differentiated, —(*a*) universals, (*b*) relations, (*c*) numbers, (*d*) truths or propositions, and (*e*) aesthetic and moral values. And of all these it can be said (*a*) that they are not sensible, (*b*) that they can, nevertheless, be conceptually grasped, and (*c*) that in some way they alone make anything, even that which exists, knowable or thinkable.

The 'plain man' would, I suppose, bluntly object to all this that nothing can *be* without existing. But, unless he can show that there is no status in reality other than the status which such things as stones and storms, trees and horses, persons and toothaches, possess, no weight can be attached to his objection.[1] A far more serious objection is that which Bertrand Russell and others have brought forward,—that if we allow there are such entities as subsistent truths, we shall have to allow likewise that there are such entities as subsistent falsehoods, and this is in itself incredible. Formidable, however, though on the surface this objection may appear to be, I do not

[1] As someone has well said, "a lively sense of reality is doubtless a salutary thing, but it has to be proved and not merely felt that a Plato's sense of reality is inferior to the ploughboy's".

think it is, in fact valid. Neither Meinong nor Husserl felt constrained to admit the being of subsistent falsehoods. And I conceive it may quite well be the case that, although there are subsistent truths, there can be falsehoods only if there are minds that make mistakes. Just as we may fall into error in regard to existing things, so we may fall into error in regard to subsisting truths. A straight stick partially immersed in water appears bent; but we do not, on that account, consider it needful to suppose that the stick actually is bent. And similarly, if it appears to an ignorant that "twice nine are sixteen", we need not suppose that there is veritably subsisting the proposition "twice nine are sixteen". That erroneous belief may well be due to the ignorant person's misapprehension of the true subsisting proposition. Accordingly, I do not conceive that the view I have been laying before you is in any way undermined by an argument of the kind just noted.

Now, I have been laying stress on the consideration that subsistent truths do not owe their reality to the circumstance that they are known or appreciated by us. The truth that $2 + 2 = 4$, or the truth that 'red differs from green', would still hold or be valid even though the surface of our planet were reduced to a frozen waste, incapable of supporting life. But can we go on to say that apart from any mind whatsoever the subsistence of truth would have any intelligible meaning? It would be, I think, excessively difficult to reply in the affirmative. A truth which no mind knows, that is simply there, uncontemplated and unthought of, would seem to lose all significance, and to be an otiose reality, what Meinong called "a home-less wanderer". Even in respect to the world of exist-ence, there is something repugnant in the notion that the vast regions of it beyond the astronomer's survey are in the position of the flowers of the field of which the poet Gray spoke "born to waste their sweetness on the desert air". By an almost irresistible persuasion, of which it is true no logical justification can be furnished, we seem driven to postulate that no portions of the realms either of existence or of truth can, in the last resort, be outside the sphere of knowledge, that no corner of the realm of reality can ultimately elude the vigilance of Mind. Indeed, the fact of finite knowledge itself would seem to involve as its ground that complete and exhaustive knowledge which the religious man ascribes to God. "The original source of the knowledge of God", it has been impressively argued, "is an experience which might be described as an experience of *not being alone in knowing the world*." From the knowledge that 'He knows' will be inferred the thesis that the unknown of nature is knowable; and the endless task of science will receive its necessary and sufficient warrant.[1]

2. The distinction upon which I have been insisting between 'existence' and 'subsistence' does not, of course, imply that there is any radical separation between these two realms of being. On the contrary, we have already seen that in regard even to mathe-matical propositions, although they depend not for their validity upon any postulate or hypothesis about existence, yet they are surprisingly exemplified in the

[1] W. E. Hocking, *The Meaning of God in Human Experience*. pp. 226–237.

world of existent fact.[1] More particularly, however, with reference to moral and aesthetic values, would I press this consideration now. It is certainly true that we are constantly ascribing value to concrete existent entities,—to sincere and fearless utterances, to deeds of rectitude and generosity, to artistic productions or appreciations of beauty, to the vigorous exercise of healthy bodily activity, and so on. These 'realizations', as we call them, we certainly do conceive as possessing value. And, unless values could be thus 'realized' in individual instances it would doubtless be inept to speak of them as subsistent entities at all. A realm of subsistent entities independent of, and unrelated to, the realm of actual existents would be incongruous and meaningless. And yet something like an antithesis of this sort is what Bertrand Russell once pictured for us in his well-known essay, entitled *The Free Man's Worship*. In that essay it was maintained that the world which science presents for our belief is "even more purposeless, more void of meaning" than the world the history of which Mephistopheles related to Dr. Faustus. Man's origin and growth, his hopes and fears, his loves and his beliefs, are, so it was conceived science has shown, but the outcome of accidental collocations of atoms. Man lives in "an alien and inhuman world", in the midst of a nature that is

[1] See *supra*, p. 201. *Cf.* Bertrand Russell, *Philosophical Essays*, p. 82: "Mathematics takes us into the region of absolute necessity, to which not only the actual world but every possible world must conform; and even here it builds a habitation, or rather finds a habitation eternally standing, where our ideals are fully satisfied and our best hopes are not thwarted. It is only when we thoroughly understand the entire independence of ourselves, which belongs to this world that reason finds, that we can adequately realize the profound importance of its beauty."

"omnipotent but blind"; and the ideals to which he does and must adhere are not 'realized' or 'realizable' in this "hostile universe".

Against a conception such as this, it is, I think, both legitimate and essential to press the consideration that constantly and persistently we do ascribe value not only to truth but to *minds* that know what is true, not only to moral ideals but to *persons* in whose lives these ideals have to some extent, at least, been 'realized', not only to ideally beautiful qualities, but to *existent objects* of nature or of art which partially, at all events, manifest those qualities. All the same, I cannot follow those writers[1] who maintain that value is not rightly to be assigned at all to ideals as such, but is only properly applicable to existing realities, or to that which is conceived as existing. It is, indeed, admitted by the writers in question that in a sense it is both true and important that particularly in our moral judgments we do acribe values to universals, and that these judgments would not be genuinely ethical otherwise. But, it is contended, it ought at once to be recognized that it is always the universal embodied *in rebus*, and not the universal either *ante res* or *post res* which has value.

To what I have already urged earlier in this lecture I need only add now one other consideration. I do not see how the position just indicated is compatible with the view that the facts of man's moral progress compel us to acknowledge that there is involved in such development an ultimate moral end or ideal,

[1] As, for instance, W. R. Sorley, *Moral Values and the Idea of God*, p. 139 *sqq.*; and A. E. Taylor, *The Faith of a Moralist*, vol. i, p. 37 *sqq.*

a morally Best which has been the spring of the practical struggle after the Better.[1] From the point of view of the finite individual, at any rate, that ideal is something not 'realized', and yet surely something which above all that he has been able to 'realize' must be said to possess value. That the supreme moral ideal is not yet but only is to be 'realized'[2] ought not, I would urge, to be regarded as constituting in the deepest sense unreality. Rather should the peculiar relation in which this ideal stands to our moral being force us to see that our ordinary view of what constitutes reality is too narrow, too limited, to stand the test of rational inspection.

3. But I am now going on to consider the ways in which values are actually exemplified in the world of concrete existence. And, first of all, let us glance at the indications which nature itself affords of the 'realization' of aesthetic values.

In a truly great sermon, Canon Mozley once observed that "Nature's ornament is but another aspect of her work; in the very act of labouring as a machine, she sleeps as a picture." Natural scenery, it is superfluous to remark, is not uniformly beautiful; but it has been significantly pointed out[3] that there is a certain level below which nature never falls. Ugly objects exist in plenty; but has anyone ever come

---

[1] Both Professor Sorley and Professor Taylor acknowledge this.

[2] By 'realizing' a value, we mean, as Professor Sorley expressed it (*ibid.*, p. 215), "the process of so modifying the nature of existents that the value becomes a feature of existing situations or persons".

[3] See C. J. Shebbeare, *The Challenge of the Universe*, 1918, p. 111 *sqq.* *Cf. The Design Argument Reconsidered*, A discussion between C. J. Shebbeare and J. McCabe, p. 6 *sqq.*

across a whole landscape or scheme of colour in nature that has descended so low as the level often reached by gaudily tinted wool-work and by coloured prints? In nature we seem invariably to encounter schemes of colour which an artist would pronounce to be in good taste, or, at least, not in bad taste. Indeed, in complaining of cheap pictures and oil-paintings we frequently express what we mean by saying that they are libels upon nature's colouring; that they are entirely out of harmony with the spirit of nature. In vases of cut flowers one may often discern discordant groupings of colour which were they as common in nature as they are in the windows of certain florists would prohibit the artist taking nature as his model, or, perhaps, render his vocation an impossibility.[1] If, then, we ask why it is that there is exemplified in our environment this wondrous indefinable essence which we call beauty, why it is that we find it scattered with such prodigality over the face of the visible world, why it is that, beyond the mere forms of material things and the ordered sequence of material events, there is this subtle spirit of beauty insinuating itself into all the processes of nature, the dawn and the sunset, the springtide freshness, the summer glory, the fading delights of autumnal fields and woods, far and wide over hill and vale, stream and sea,—if we ask questions such as these, does not the

[1] *Cf.* S. S. Laurie, *Synthetica*, vol. ii, p. 146: "Some would seem to hold that Aesthetics, that is to say the philosophy of the Beautiful, is to be sought and found in Art. My interpretation of experience generally does not allow me to accept this restriction. If I am to find the explanation of the Beautiful in the creations of Art, I must first know what I mean by the Beautiful in Nature."

answer seem well-nigh irresistible that it is because
a supreme artist has been at work and been 'realizing'
in the realm of existent fact these ideals of beauty
and sublimity?

That answer has been contested on various grounds.
One such contention, still widely prevalent, has been
that the aspects of beauty and sublimity which we
recognize in nature, 'tertiary qualities', as Bosanquet
named them, are not, in fact, features of nature at
all, but are purely subjective characteristics, characteristics which we as percipients read into, import into,
nature, and which are not there as objective realities.
I am not going to enter here upon an elaborate
criticism of this view. Whoever holds, as I do, that
so-called 'secondary qualities'—colours, sounds and
the rest—are no mere 'ideas in us', as Locke maintained, but are, on the contrary, actual properties of
material things, is bound, it seems to me, to admit
that the 'tertiary qualities' are likewise no subjective
ideas of ours, are no less certainly ingredients of
nature than extension, figure and motion. I shall be
content now, however, with laying stress upon two
considerations. (a) If the human mind in some
mysterious fashion throws up from the depths of its
being those aspects of beauty and sublimity which
it seems to discern in nature, think of the anomalous
position of such a mind stationed in the midst of an
environment utterly foreign to what it itself produces.
How is it conceivable that a mind, so circumstanced,
could, by means of 'natural selection' or by any other
process, have acquired the marvellous facility of
inventing appearances of beauty, of clothing the

outward world with them, whilst that world itself is altogether devoid of the attributes thus assigned to it? Such a mind in such an environment would be in a worse predicament than Robinson Crusoe on his desert island. (b) Again, what would become of aesthetic appreciation itself if the artist or the poet were once persuaded that the grandeur and the serenity which he had taken to be features of the scene around are, in truth, illusions, fictitious fancies, of his own fertile imagination? If, for instance, on that auspicious occasion when "magnificent the morning rose, in memorable pomp, glorious as e'er he had beheld", the reflexion had dawned upon the youthful Wordsworth that after all the magnificence was not there in the vast landscape he was then contemplating, but had been simply conjured up by himself, would he have emerged from that experience with the assurance of being a "dedicated Spirit"? Did he not, indeed, claim for poetry that it was "the breath and finer spirit of all knowledge, the impassioned expression which is on the face of all science"? In point of fact, at the root of the inspiration of every great artistic genius there has lain the conviction that—

> "Nature is made better by no mean,
> But Nature makes that mean; so o'er the Art,
> Which you say adds to Nature, is an Art
> That Nature makes."

Once more, it has become customary to urge that the beauty of nature is largely due to purely natural or utilitarian causes. Thus, Darwin sought to account for the tasteful schemes of colour in the plant and animal world by resort to the theory of natural selection. Flowers "have been rendered conspicuous in contrast with the green leaves, and in consequence at the same time beautiful, so that they can be easily observed by insects". He had come to this conclusion from finding it an invariable rule that when a flower is fertilized by the wind it never has a gaily coloured corolla. So, too, a great number of male animals and birds, and a host of magnificently coloured butterflies, owe their beauty, he maintained, to sexual selection, —to the fact, namely, that the more beautiful males have been continually preferred by the females. It is, however, obvious that, even though this explanation be accepted, the beauty of inanimate nature would still remain unaccounted for. But, although I am not a biologist, I venture to doubt whether Darwin, in this instance, really made out his case. It is not the mere brightness, not the mere brilliancy or conspicuousness, of the colouring of birds and butterflies and flowers that is in question; it is the harmoniousness, the delicacy, the gracefulness, of the schemes of colour thus exhibited that calls to be explained. We can scarcely suppose that a nicety of taste in this respect which is rare even among human beings is a common property of insects and female butterflies!

So far, then, it would appear that those who reject a spiritual view of the universe have no alternative but to attribute beauty in nature to accident or chance. But now I would ask, is it not part of the charm which we ascribe to beauty in nature that it seems, at least, to be expressive of meaning, of thought, of design? No one can read and enter into the spirit of the first book of *The Prelude*, for instance, without recognizing that this belief lay, at any rate, at the root of its author's inspiration. Now, in respect to human works of art there can be little doubt that the value we attach to them is largely dependent upon the fact that we do take them to be revelations of the minds of their artists. Could we be persuaded that, let us say, the Venus of Milo originated in some incomprehensible fashion from the working of blind mechanical agencies we should be disposed, I imagine, to regard it as wondrous or surprising rather than as beautiful. Is it really otherwise with respect to the beauties of nature? Can we consistently lay down one rule for artistic beauty and quite another for natural beauty? If, in order rightly to appreciate the former, we need to contemplate the mind of the artist beyond his work, are we not, in order rightly to appreciate the latter, likewise impelled to contemplate the artist beyond his work? In short, what I am suggesting is that were naturalism, in the lower sense of the term (to use Pringle-Pattison's phrase), to become the dominating creed of civilized mankind, delight in the beauties of nature, if it survived at all, would be shorn of more than half its spontaneity and fervour.

4. If, however, the foregoing argument should appear to be, to some extent, inconclusive, a more convincing line of reflexion comes into view when we have regard to moral values. And here I propose to ask, in the first place, whether we can be satisfied that moral ideals are no mere subjective preferences of ours or devices that are useful for social life, but are objectively valid; and, in the second place, whether

we can regard the world in which we are stationed as a fitting environment for the 'realization' of those ideals.

The most direct way of making manifest the fact that moral ideals are no mere subjective constructions of our own is, perhaps, to ask ourselves the question which Kant put in the forefront of his ethical inquiry, —the question, namely, as to what the notion of duty or moral obligation really involves. It clearly rests upon and is devoid of content without the postulate that in human nature, in human life, the desirable, as distinguished from the desired, is not exhausted in the mere potentiality of being pleased or gratified. It implies, that is to say, that the good for a moral agent need not necessarily be such as to afford in his life continuous pleasure or gratification. But it implies much more than this. The kind of obligation prescribed by the law of duty is *unconditional* in character, and it may well stand in opposition to all those varying conditions on which the pleasure or happiness of the individual from moment to moment depends. Indeed, so soon as there is the possibility, on the part of a self-conscious subject, of reflexion upon his life as a whole, so soon as it becomes possible for him to contemplate pleasure or happiness as depending on conditions of his temporal existence, then he is constrained to conceive of the moral end as differing from, as being even opposed to, the conception of happiness.[1] Further, it is a prerequisite of duty that the self-conscious

---

[1] This characteristic is no other than what received such remarkable recognition from J. S. Mill when he was dealing with qualitative distinction among pleasures.

subject should be a free agent. Kant has shown, once
for all, that freedom is an essential category of morality.
For no rational being can regard his actions as due to
external compulsion; and, consequently, he can only
act under the idea of freedom, or be for practical
purposes free. In other words, in acting a conscious
self invariably ascribes its action to itself, and it could
not ascribe its action to itself if it did not derive from
itself a principle for determining its conduct. In short,
Kant was virtually maintaining that a self which is
aware of itself as free or self-determining is *ipso facto*
free, is *ipso facto* self-determining. Not even the moral
law is thrust or forced upon us; it bears with it
the characteristic of being obligatory, it does not
bear the characteristic of being overwhelmingly
powerful.

In the light of these considerations, let us further
inspect the consciousness of "ought". In ordinary
conversation, it is true, we often employ the term in
a merely conventional manner, and then it does not
carry with it the sense of a binding constraint. "I ought
to go to town, in order to attend to a matter of business", "I ought to consult a doctor, if my health does
not improve", "I ought to give pleasure to my friends",
—we are frequently in the habit of expressing ourselves in language of this kind. But, in these instances,
the lines of action indicated are not such as the moral
law prescribes. On the contrary, they are what Kant
called "counsels of prudence"; they are not good in
themselves, they are good only as means to ends
which there is no imperative necessity to will at all.
When, however, we *do* use the term "ought" in the

strict sense in which Kant was using it we must mean that there *is* a necessity to will, that the obligation laid upon us *is* unconditional and not one of our choosing. There are doubtless occasions when, as in the well-known case of Jeanie Deans, it is clearly permissible not to speak the truth to an individual who questions us; but there certainly are occasions when we are conscious that we ought to speak the truth whatever happens, let the consequences be what they may. And then we do not ask why we should speak the truth; we recognize, at least implicitly, that such a question would only have a meaning on an assumption which would be destructive of the moral purity of our conduct. If, now, we are repeatedly encountering behests of this intrinsically imperative character, how are we to account for so significant a fact? Kant's answer to this question is sufficiently familiar. We can, he averred, only account for it by recognizing that man is a denizen of two worlds,—a natural world and a spiritual (or, as he expressed it, an 'intelligible') world. While one may well hesitate in accepting Kant's view of the constitution of these two worlds, yet in essence, I venture to urge, his answer is alone adequate to the facts. Unless duty, as he conceived it, be a phantom of unreality,—unless it be a delusion from which the fortunate lower animals escape,—its ultimate source of initiative must be sought in a realm beyond the sensuous; and this means that the human soul must be enveloped in a supernatural environment.

5. Moral ideals are, then, essentially objective and the notion that the moral law is in any way constituted, or rendered authoritative, by subjective acts on the

part of human agents calls to be unreservedly rejected. In genuinely moral conduct, as we have seen, the agent pursues, or endeavours to 'realize', ends or ideals in virtue of their own intrinsic worth, and not on account of any extraneous advantages to which they may be thought to lead. But it remains further to note that these various moral ideals are not to be conceived as isolated or as independent of one another; they must necessarily form a coherent system. In other words, there must be, as, at the beginning of the *Ethics*, Aristotle is to be found insisting, one ultimate end, one final good, that embraces or constitutes the several goods. This 'final good' is not, indeed, to be contemplated as a mere sum of specific goods, but rather as that in reference to which these latter have their place and value. Now, from the very nature of the case, it must clearly be impossible for the human subject, at any stage in his career, to depict the content of this 'ultimate good' in all its fullness and richness. "We cannot describe the goal of our pilgrimage" simply "because we have never reached it." No ethical theory ever put forward contains in its statement of the 'final end' other than general characteristics of what is therein included. So far, therefore, from thinking it a defect in any representation of the supreme moral end that there should be a want of definiteness in regard to the various features involved in it, it appears to me that only as being 'formal', in this sense, is a 'final end' conceivable by us at all. Such a conception cannot be other than 'formal', and for a two-fold reason. On the one hand, it can indicate only the common or universal characteristics which must be exhibited by any concrete mode of conduct falling within the scope of the conception of duty; and, on the other hand, it has inevitably the indefiniteness that must attach to our conception of an ideal as compared with our representations of accomplished facts. Nevertheless, just in so far as the struggle after a Better has been animated by the idea of there being a Best, we *do* know enough of the latter to guide our conduct; "enough", in T. H. Green's words, "to judge whether the prevailing interests which make our character are or are not in the direction which tends further to realize the capabilities of the human spirit".

What, then, is the status of this ideal in the universe of reality? Can we look upon it as simply there, as somehow subsisting in its own right, so to speak, and as needing nothing beyond itself to account for its presence? We have seen how incongruous it would be to regard the realm of truth in its entirety as simply subsisting apart from a Mind by whom it is apprehended and known. But here we are face to face with an ideal which admittedly no finite mind has fully grasped, but which is none the less valid although it is not yet 'realized' nor even discernible by us in all its completeness. I do not say, as some have said, that the moral ideal must exist in the mind of God, because as an ideal it does not seem to me to be an existent, either in a mind or elsewhere. I would, however, submit that only on the assumption of the existence of a Mind by whom it is known in its entirety and on whom its reality is dependent can we rationally think of this ideal as subsisting at all. An absolute moral law is conceivable only on the supposition that it has its ground in an existent Being who is supremely good.

But here, in this connexion, the further question arises, the question whether the natural world affords the possibility of 'realizing' the ideals which we have been calling moral, whether it is a fitting field for the development of a being whose conduct is animated by moral principles. Or, has man been placed in a universe in which his striving towards the good is doomed to frustration? In seriously facing this question, we are driven, I think, at once to see that the ethical theory known as hedonism is incompatible with the conception of a wise and righteous God. For the world-order is obviously not adjusted to the purpose of providing a maximum of pleasure or happiness for conscious beings, nor even to the purpose of distributing pleasure or happiness equally among them. No fact of experience can be more patent than that nature is very inadequately adapted to the desires of the pleasure-seeker; "the course of nature", as Hume expressed it, "tends not to human or animal felicity", and is, therefore, "not established for that purpose". Moreover, in this world goodness and happiness are by no manner of means necessarily conjoined. The workers of iniquity often flourish; pain and misery are the lot of the saint as well as of the sinner. If, however, the ethical end be not pleasure or happiness, but what we have been taking it to be, goodness, or let us say moral excellence, the story is otherwise. Opportunities of doing the duties that lie nearest for duty's sake alone and in the genuine moral spirit are afforded abundantly in every sphere of life and in all

kinds of material and social surroundings; these deeds
need only the good will and are not dependent upon
circumstances. Be the circumstances as they may,
there is always an attitude towards them in which
what is good can be 'realized', and in 'realizing' which
the human spirit can attain satisfaction. Not only so.
Pain and suffering are no insuperable obstacles to the
moral order of the world; on the contrary, they may
even be regarded as subserving that order. Certainly,
the noblest of souls have passed through seas of
tribulation and have been made perfect by suffering.
In truth, a moral character is largely formed by
encountering and surmounting obstacles; and it may
well be that hardness of circumstance and strain of
conflict are needful for the growth and nurture of
moral beings.

Furthermore, even a cursory survey of the history
of civilized mankind is sufficient to convince us that,
although morality in every age and country emanates
from the same root, it is never stationary. And, as
T. H. Green has conclusively shown, moral progress
has consisted not only in the widening of the range
of persons whose common good is sought, but also
in a gradually more exhaustive determination of the
contents of what is described as good. There is no
doubt that morality has at all times exhibited one
uniform feature. There has always been present to
human consciousness some conception of the ideal of
conduct, or of an end to which the individual thinks
his conduct must needs conform, and on this account
it would seem natural that the terms for the several
typical virtues should retain a certain uniformity. But,

with increase in the complexity of life, with increasing insight into what is necessary in conduct in order to 'realize' the ideal, there goes a change in the conception of the ideal itself. So that he who now calls for temperance or righteousness in action means by it something indefinitely more complicated and comprehensive than could have been contemplated by a thinker of an earlier age. To a very large extent each stage of moral progress has been effected through the influence and teaching of some personality who has been gifted with a richness of character and depth of insight beyond what is possessed by his contemporaries. These great personalities in history, when closely studied, exhibit just those marks which we can assign to the pressure of the ideal, to the influence of the ideal on human life and action. The true moral reformer might be described as 'the child of the ideal' while the majority around him are 'children of the *status quo*'.

It has, indeed, often been objected to this interpretation of the great personalities who have been exponents of the ideals of humanity that when we scrutinize their careers sufficiently we can discover in them so much of individual concern, so much of self-seeking, and so little purely disinterested, that we must rather assign the effects produced to the accidents of such self-seeking than to the pressure of the ideal. This objection in one form or another has been frequently urged in the case of those who have received from history the title of martyrs. In the discussions which have been carried on concerning the nature of martyrdom there has often been advanced the argument that, since in these men there was invariably to be found the belief that a life of blessedness awaited them hereafter, their action amounted to nothing else than a finer form of self-interest. In this reference, however, let me lay before you two short extracts from Fichte's Lectures on *The Characteristics of the Present Age*. "Should anyone offer this objection that they, indeed, sacrificed the present life in the expectation of an infinitely higher, heavenly, and blessed life, which they hoped to deserve by these sacrifices and sufferings; and, therefore, that it was still but enjoyment for enjoyment, and indeed a lesser for a greater,—then I would entreat such an objector earnestly to consider the following. How inadequately soever these men might express themselves in words regarding the blessedness of another world, and with what sensuous pictures soever they might clothe their descriptions of this happiness, I ask only to know how they arrived at this firm Faith in another world, which they attested so nobly by their deeds; and what this Faith, as an act of mind, really is. Does not the mind that faithfully accepts another world as certain, in this very acceptance renounce the present one?— and is not this Faith itself the sacrifice, once and for ever accomplished and perfected in the mind, and which only manifests itself outwardly when special circumstances call it forth? Let it be no wonder, then, that they willingly sacrificed everything to their belief in an Eternal life, for, if they did so, does not the wonder remain that they *did believe*; in which belief the egoist, who is incapable of letting the present escape, even for a moment, from his view, can never

follow or approach them." . . . "It is honour, someone
may say, which inspires the hero,—the burning image
of fame in after times, which impels him through
difficulties and dangers, and which repays him for a
life of sacrifice and self-denial, in the coin on which
he sets most value. I answer, even if it should be so,
what then is this honour? Whence arises this thought
of the judgment which others may pass upon us, the
judgment of future generations whose praise or blame
shall echo over our graves unheard;—whence has it
acquired this amazing power which enables it to
suppress and extinguish the personal life of the hero?
Is it not obvious that in the depths of his mind there
lies the principle that only on one condition can his
life be of value to him, can even be endurable by him,
—on this, namely, that the voices of mankind at large
shall concur in ascribing value to it? Is not this very
thought of the race and of its judgment on the individual an admission that the race alone is entitled to
pass the final judgment on true merit? Is it not at the
same time the supposition that this final judgment
must be grounded on the inquiry whether the individual
has or has not devoted himself to the race?—and is
it not the silent, respectful acquiescence in the judgment proceeding on these premises?—in a word, is
not this thought precisely that on which we have
based the life according to reason?"[1]

Taken generally, the objection is, in fact, but a
special form of that tendency to oppose to one another
the several factors of the moral life which has affected
so injuriously the course of ethical inquiry. To set

[1] *Sämmtliche Werke*, Bd. 7, pp. 46 and 50.

over against one another the concrete fullness of human life and the bare abstraction of duty as such was the cardinal error in Kant's procedure. It is only through the conjunction of the thought of the ideal with feeling and impulse that morality becomes a real fact and ceases to be a mere abstraction. It is, therefore, inevitable that even in the most heroic life there will be found those elements of personal feeling and individual impulse that are peculiar, not to the conception of the ideal, but to the individual life on which the ideal exerts its influence. That is but a poor analysis which would tend to destroy the character of the ideal because that ideal can only be accepted and wrought out in the life of the individual. I think, then, it may be rightly said in regard to these heroic personalities that the ideal was in truth the essential influence, and that they were distinguished from others not merely by force of character and power of action but by the relatively greater share which the ideal played in determining their lives.

PANTHEISM AND THEISM

IN this concluding lecture I propose to consider one of the more fundamental issues of speculative philosophy, an issue which is still a very real one in present-day reflexion. And I can lead up to the subject I have in view by dwelling first of all upon an argument to prove the existence of God which we have not yet discussed, and which in one form or another has largely influenced philosophic thought.

1. Expressed concisely, the argument I refer to is to the effect that the outlook on truth and beauty and goodness which man has attained itself implies the cardinal principle of theism. For the *possibilities* of human thought cannot exceed the *actuality* of real existence; the best we think, or can think, must at least be. Such is the gist of the so-called 'ontological argument', which meets us at the beginning of the period it is usual to describe as that of modern philosophy. It was first formulated by the great Christian theologian, Archbishop Anselm. Anselm tried, namely, to show that the existence of God is *immediately* evident, and that doubt of God's existence is only possible so long as we do not realize the

meaning of the term 'God'. Whoever uses that term intelligently must, he contended, at least conceive of God as the greatest of beings; for, unless God be conceived as the greatest of beings, there would be no genuine thought of God at all. But, in this case, the predicate 'greatest' virtually involves 'existence'; because God would not be the greatest being conceivable were He a mere idea in a finite mind, and not also an actual entity. For then we *should* be able to think of a being greater than God; of a Being, namely, who was not only *thought of* by us, but who was also really existent.

This argument was speedily called in question by the aged monk Gaunilo, who, in a quaint little tract, came to the rescue of 'the fool who said in his heart there is no God'. The argument would only be valid, so Gaunilo insisted, if it could be shown that the fool could not understand the meaning of the assertion that 'God exists' without recognizing, at the same time, that this assertion is true; and that was precisely what Anselm had *not* shown. Gaunilo sought to clench his criticism by means of a celebrated illustration. Imagine, he suggested, an island in the ocean, which may be called a lost island, inasmuch as no one has been able to find it,—an island of the blessed, richer, more fertile, lovelier than any actual island we know of. If such an island were described to us, we should understand readily enough the meaning of the words,—the lost island would be, that is to say, *in our thought* after the manner in which God is in the thought of the fool. Yet it would be nonsense to contend that the island must likewise exist somewhere in the ocean, seeing that otherwise it would not be what, by definition it is, more excellent and perfect than any other spot on earth.

Anselm replied that the lost island was no true parallel; that there was, in fact, *no* parallel to the instance with which he was concerned. Whoever thinks of the greatest of beings as non-existent *is* thinking a contradiction, because he is thinking of the 'greatest of beings' as less than what can be conceived, namely, as less than a 'greatest of beings' that exists. So far, no doubt, Anselm's reply was, if not conclusive, at least pertinent. But what he had not shown was that this phrase 'the greatest of beings' had any definite meaning whatsoever. To urge, as he did, that even the 'fool' must understand the meaning of the words before he can deny that they stand for a real existent is, in fact, unavailing. On the same ground, he would have had to say that 'round squares' and 'unicorns' exist, seeing that obviously I can make assertions about them, as when I say 'there are no such things as round squares', 'there are no such things as unicorns'. Must, then, 'round squares' and 'unicorns' necessarily be in my thought before I can assert these propositions? By no means. It may be that my ground for asserting these propositions is that 'round squares' and 'unicorns' are merely words which have no intelligible meaning. So too 'the greatest of beings' may be simply a phrase to which no intelligible meaning can be ascribed,—that is to say, there may be in the mind no 'idea' of it at all.

In a somewhat different form, the same argument reappears in Descartes' *Meditations*. That God exists follows at once, so Descartes maintained, from the idea we have of the divine nature. We have, namely, the idea of an absolutely complete and infinite being; and from that we can deduce with unhesitating certainty that existence must be one of the attributes or characteristics of that being. For it is no less impossible to conceive of a being absolutely complete and infinite, yet wanting the characteristic of existence, than to conceive of a triangle while denying the equality of its angles to two right angles. Just as equality of its angles to two right angles is involved in the *idea* of a triangle, so is existence involved in the *idea* of God.

In his well-known refutation of the Cartesian argument, Kant used an illustration similar to that which had been used by Gaunilo. There is, he insisted, a very considerable difference between the idea of three hundred thalers in my mind and the existence of three hundred thalers in my purse. If, as Descartes had alleged, existence is involved in infinite completeness, then certainly the *idea* of an infinitely complete being must include the *idea* of that being's existence. But the presence in our mind of the *idea* of existence proves in no way the *actuality* of such existence.

The really vital point in Kant's criticism consisted in his contention that existence can never be a characteristic or attribute of any apprehended object, after the manner in which yellowish or squareness may be. An existent is that which has attributes or qualities; or, as he expressed it, existence can never form part, as qualities, or properties, do, of the content of a notion. Of the importance of this contention I shall have more to say presently. But, first of all, it will be well to point out that the Cartesian argument is not so readily disposed of as Kant seemed to suppose it could be. For, after all, to use a phrase of one of the Post-Kantian writers, God is something very different from islands and thalers; and Descartes himself had expressly affirmed, as Anselm had previously affirmed, that it was *only* in reference to the idea of the Infinite that his argument had any significance. This is an idea the content of which is wholly inexplicable by reference to finite and, therefore, limited facts; and, accordingly, its mere presence in our consciousness is sufficient to establish the existence of a reality corresponding to it. Indications are not wanting in Descartes' writings of the view, afterwards developed by Spinoza, that the infinite reality is itself actually operative in our thinking and is not present there merely as an *idea*. He insisted, for example, on the primordial and positive character of infinitude; it was not something which we get at negatively by leaving out the limitations attaching to what is finite; on the contrary, it was prior to, and the basis of, our knowledge of the finite and particular.

2. At the same time, even though it be admitted that the Infinite is thus involved in all our thinking, we are certainly *not* entitled, on that ground alone, to conclude that the one infinite reality is a self-conscious mind. In point of fact, the Cartesian philosophy reached its culmination in the pantheistic metaphysic of Spinoza, according to which finite things and finite minds were, like waves of the sea, but modes or

modifications of the ultimate substance, and had no independent existence of their own.

3. But I want more particularly to consider a line of reflexion in which a strenuous attempt *is* made so to determine the nature of absolute being, which we may say the ontological argument constrains us to recognize, as to avoid the pantheistic terminus just indicated. Spinoza's initial mistake, Hegel contended, was to define the Absolute as Substance and not as Subject. According to Hegel's view, the ultimate ground or principle of all reality is not mere Substance, which in itself is bare of all determinations, but Mind or Spirit, an infinite Self-consciousness, which differentiates itself into the multiplicity of material things and mental lives. Does this change, however, really succeed in surmounting the pantheism of Spinoza?

Note, at the outset, what exactly the change implies. Thought is no longer regarded as 'something which exists side by side with things'. Rather was Thought to be conceived as that which embraces and comprises them all, which projects them, so to speak, from itself. An infinite Mind, whose mode of being is at once consciousness of self and constitutive of what is other than self,—in some such way might one briefly delineate Hegel's mode of viewing the whole of reality. The Absolute Intelligence, as Thought or Reason, or the ultimate spiritual principle, externalizes its own essence, gives rise thus to its own objects; and, as the content of the Absolute Thought, the objective world remains eternally within the unity of the one supreme Self-consciousness. According, then, to this vast process of Spiritualization, all things are cast from one mould; the temporal process which goes on in the world is but the counterpart, or the manifestation, of the thought-development of God. "Thoughts", so Hegel tells us, "do not stand between us and things, shutting us off from things; they rather shut us together with them." Nature, in other words, is to be viewed as a system of objective thoughts—a system which thus forms a connected organic whole, and is consequently interpretable in terms of thought itself. And finite minds are 'reproductions',—to use T. H. Green's term—of the universal Mind; it is truer to say not that we think, but that thought goes on in us. Thought is not, therefore, a peculiar characteristic of man; it is the presence in man of the universal intellect, the light that lighteth everyone that cometh into the world. "We recognize in Nature's inner being only our own reason and feel ourselves at home there." Spirit has the certainty which Adam had when he saw Eve: "This is flesh of my flesh and bone of my bone."

4. The fascination of a line of reflexion such as this is sufficiently manifest. From a mere examination of the simplest act of knowing, it seems to furnish us at one bound with a spiritual view of the universe. But further inspection will, I think, convince us that we are here still within the meshes of a pantheism, from which the mere substitution of Spirit, regarded as Hegel regarded it, for Substance, does not afford a means of escape. The realm of reality is, in truth, vastly too complex to fit into the simple framework here provided for it. Over and over again, for instance, Hegel was compelled to admit the presence of what he

himself described as 'contingency' in the sphere of nature that obstinately refused to accommodate itself to his logical scheme. For him nature was always very much a kind of step-child. And hence, too, it is easily explicable that he was never very happy when dealing with the mental life of man. For when nature is thus transformed into a tissue of thought-contents and relations, the mental life of man must fall into line with the rest; individual souls must be viewed as compliant tools in the working out of the logical machinery. As Principal Oman has very truly said, "in the end real history has no place in Hegel's intellectual construction. What masquerades as history is a show staged by dialectic".[1] In short, the attempt to spiritualize everything has had here the effect of de-spiritualizing even that which is ordinarily recognized as spiritual. I want to justify this contention somewhat more in detail. But, first of all, let me try to show that the basal position on which this system of thought is made to rest will not bear the weight that is reposed upon it.

Briefly that position may be said to be this. An object, it is assumed, can only exist in relation to and in distinction from a subject; neither can be conceived as real apart from the other. And the consequence is at once drawn that there can be no natural world except such as is relative to and dependent upon a subject-mind that thinks it or is aware of it. But there is a vicious fallacy in such reasoning. No doubt, if you define an 'object' as that which stands over against and is apprehended by a 'subject', it is true that there

[1] *The Natural and the Supernatural*, p. 291.

can be no 'object' apart from a 'subject', for so much
has then been implied by the very terms you are using.
That an 'object' apart from a 'subject' is impossible
is, in that case, no less obvious than that it is impossible
there can be a husband without a wife. For these are
correlative terms, and the one implies the other. Yet,
as Hume acutely argued in another context, though
husbands without wives are nonsense, that does not
amount to saying that every man is married. And so,
too, though 'objects' without 'subjects' are absurd,
that does not amount to saying that everything, every
material thing, must be an 'object', or that when it
is an 'object' it cannot exist except as in that relation.
This is precisely what needs to be proved if the system
in question is to stand.

But more important for our purpose is it to make
clear another consideration. The conception, namely,
of ultimate Thought which we have been inspecting
by no means involves the *thinking* of a self-conscious
existing mind; it is rather Thought as consisting of
a complex of timeless entities, such as we mean when
we speak of a 'system of thought' or a 'body of knowledge'. And this conception of Thought, as consisting
of timeless contents, you will find to be characteristic
of all the writers who have followed in the footsteps
of Hegel. They have practically ignored the *process*
or *activity* of thinking, as it takes place in an actually
existing mental life, and they have confined their
attention to what I have called thought-contents—
that is to say, the truths thought about. They have
fallen, it seems to me, into the error of identifying
truth and existence. For instance, in predicating

'timelessness' of the 'eternal consciousness', T. H. Green was virtually making that identification. Strange to say, he himself drew attention to the ambiguity attending the use of all such terms as knowledge, experience, perception, and the like, "which may", as he put it, "denote events in our mental history as well as that *of which* in those states we are conscious, the content and object of consciousness". Yet, after having emphasized this fundamental distinction, he appears, in developing his view, to have completely missed its significance. Now, as we have seen, truth, in common with other values, certainly does possess the characteristic of timelessness. But the features of timelessness, invariability, universality, which belong to the contents of truth are not features of existing fact; all existing facts are temporal facts, subject to change and variability. Truths can, of course, only be known by a knowing mind; but the *knowing* is not, on that account, timeless equally with the truth *known*. That would mean that a truth is known by a truth. And yet Green proceeds at once from the conception of the timelessness of the contents of truth to the conception of the timelessness of what he calls 'the eternal consciousness', which he evidently *wants* to contemplate as a knowing mind. The 'eternal consciousness' is, he tells us, a 'combining and relating *activity*'; yet this 'combining and relating activity' is declared by him to be 'unchanging, identical, independent of time'. You have here, it seems to me, a plainly illegitimate procedure, on Green's part. No *activity* can be timeless; a 'timeless *activity*' is simply a contradiction in terms. If the 'eternal consciousness' is veritably to be conceived as 'timeless', then it is being conceived as a logical system of truth, such a system of truth as Plato meant by the realm of Ideas, which Plato certainly did not identify with God.

5. And, in the connexion, I am puzzled by certain of the contentions of Professor Taylor in his Gifford Lectures to which I have more than once referred. Professor Taylor is very far from being a follower of Hegel, but in regard to the question we are now discussing he appears to me to oscillate between two conflicting positions. On the one hand, when he speaks of God as 'the *concrete* unity of all good',[1] as 'the *efficient* as well as the exemplary cause of the whole moral life',[2] as 'the author and sustainer of moral effort',[3] and so on, he certainly seems to be contemplating the Deity as an actual self-conscious mind; indeed, he speaks of God as 'a person of supreme excellence'.[4] Such a mind can doubtless in one sense be said to transcend time—in the sense, namely, that its knowledge of truth would be exhaustive and entire—but not in the sense of *existing* timelessly. On the other hand, when Professor Taylor insists that in God the distinction between essence and existence is transcended, that God *is* the 'supreme value',[5] he seems to be occupying Hegelian ground. The 'eternity' which he pronounces to be 'the form' of the divine life he then describes as an 'abiding present', as that which has no element of successiveness, no before or after, connected with it.[6] "There must be", he tells us,

[1] *The Faith of a Moralist*, vol. i, p. 101.
[2] *ibid.*, p. 139.   [3] *ibid.*   [4] *ibid.*, p. 207.
[5] *ibid.*, vol. ii, p. 147.   [6] *ibid.*, vol. i, p. 426.

"a *prius* and *posterius* in the world as apprehended by
God. But there is no *prius* or *posterius* in God, or in
God's *apprehension* of the world. The whole process,
prius and *posterius* alike, would fall for God, who
never becomes but is, within a single present."[1] I am
sure Professor Taylor has a definite conception of
what he is here trying to say, but I find myself left
gasping when I attempt to put the parts of this statement together. In the first place, to talk of a 'present'
at all, except in correlation with a past and a future,
appears to be strangely incongruous. And, in the
second place, I would urge, that, however comprehensive an act of apprehension may be, yet, as an *act*,
it must occupy a period of time and be thus differentiated from other acts of apprehension. As, indeed,
Professor Taylor himself elsewhere puts it, "every
conscious act fills an actual interval".

In another part of his work, Professor Taylor brings
forward an illustration to exemplify what he means in
the connexion just referred to. He tries to show that,
in so far as ideal values are apprehended or appropriated
at all, they affect the nature of him who apprehends
and appropriates them; his temporal character is, to
a certain extent, obliterated, and takes on, so to speak,
the form of 'eternity'. And he instances some familiar
experiences which seem to him confirmations of this
view. For example, when one is enjoying, with heart
and soul, a symphony of Beethoven, and is thoroughly
engrossed by it, that symphony occupies the *total*
field of his awareness, and a real musician would be
conscious of a whole 'movement' as present all at

[1] *The Faith of a Moralist*, vol. i, p. 427.

once and not as coming to him piecemeal. Now, I do not doubt, for a moment, the reality of experiences such as these. We all know how curiously, in certain situations, the consciousness of past and future may fall away, and how we may become absorbed, as it were, in what, using Professor Taylor's mode of expression, may legitimately enough be described as an *abiding now*. In thus apprehending the timeless, we may, it is quite true, become oblivious of the flow of time. Yes; but time is flowing, all the same, and our oblivious-ness of the fact does *not* imply that the actual processes of the mental life—the processes, namely, of perceiv-ing, thinking, feeling and willing—have, in any way, ceased to be temporal processes, or that the mental life, as an existent, has itself been transformed into a timeless entity, or has even, in Professor Taylor's phraseology, taken on 'the form of eternity'. No; a supposition of that sort is due, I cannot but think, to a confusion between two essentially different things —the act, namely, of knowing *and* that which is thereby known. What is 'eternal' or timeless cannot, obviously, be known except by a knowing mind; but from that truism it does not follow that the knowing is itself 'timeless' in the sense in which that which is known may be. On the contrary, the knowing, as a mental fact, is an activity; and, consequently, a temporal event; it occurs or happens at a particular stage in the history of an individual mind. A knower who knows, but does not know *at* any period, or *through* any period, of time, is, in short, a contradictory notion.

It is only fair to add that Professor Taylor ack-nowledges that, in the case of any finite mind, the transcendence of time, which he thinks he has thus illustrated, is only very partially approximated to, and is never really accomplished. So far as a finite mind is concerned, he fully allows that the distinction between *existence* and *essence*, between that which has qualities or attributes and the qualities or attributes themselves, is vital and important. And, of course, as an *existent*, the finite mind is *in time*. But he argues, following in this respect, the lead of St. Thomas, in God the distinction between *existence* and *essence* must fall away. God can have no 'nature' or 'essence' distinguishable from, and making itself felt through, the phases of His actual existence. Here, and here only, the distinction between *essence* and *existence* would have no meaning; and, consequently, the distinction between an attribute and that which is the subject of the attribute would be meaningless also. Of the divine Being we can say, as of nothing else, that it *is* its own goodness. Its goodness is not adjectival to it, because in it it is all one *to be* and *to be good*. And, therefore, since goodness is timeless, so also must God, who is identical with goodness, be likewise timeless.

This is doubtless orthodox Thomist doctrine, but it has always appeared to me to be singularly unconvincing, and, indeed, to evince itself, on careful scrutiny, as unintelligible. If God be identical with His goodness, I presume we must also say that God is identical with His love, with His knowledge, with His insight, and so on. And that would mean that God's love and knowledge and insight are one and the same. Well, if anyone is prepared to maintain that thesis, I am afraid anything I could say would be unavailing. But the main point I would emphasize is that God, so conceived, is no longer a living, operative self-conscious mind; He is then pictured as just that timeless whole of thought-contents of which I have already spoken.

6. What I have been urging becomes, I think, still more strikingly evident when we turn to a conception widely current, although I do not intend to impute it to Professor Taylor—the conception, namely, of finite minds as parts of or included in the absolute or universal Mind. As an example of the sort of relation that is meant reference is frequently made to what is to be found in a social system. The community, so it is contended, may be said to be a single mind, and its members partial phases or modes of it. 'The communal will is a single thing as much as external nature, which is revealed in the same way. Participation in its structure makes every particular unit an individual, that is, a particular in which the universal or the identity assumes a special modification. His will is made out of the common substance.'[1] Society, that is to say, is a whole of which its individual members are parts. Now, we may admit, at once, that the life of a community has a certain unity and identity of its own. This unity and identity is, however, essentially different from that of an individual mind. In so far as the individual is a member of society, his mental processes are obviously not connected with those of the other members in a way at all analogous to that in which the various phases and processes of his own being are

[1] Bernard Bosanquet, *Proceedings of Aristotelian Society*, N.S. vol. xviii, 1918, p. 499.

connected in the unity of his self-conscious life. If A knows that one side of a globe represents the old continent and B knows that the other side represents the new, they do not, *therefore*, either individually or both together, know that the old continent forms one side and the new continent the other. Unity of apperception, as Kant called it, would be absent. A may, of course, communicate to B what B does not know. Yet this merely signifies that A uses means whereby B is enabled to know *for himself* the same fact that is already known to A. When it is known to each of them, its being known to A is distinct from its being known to B, and A's awareness that B knows it is *not* the awareness that he knows it himself. "Social interrelations consist," to use the apt words of Professor Stout, "in the mutual knowledge of each other and mutual interest in each other of distinct minds, and in their co-operation in thinking and willing. The essential presupposition is that the mutually co-operating minds are distinct individuals, and not merely parts or phases of one mind. There is nothing in the social system which thinks or feels or wills, except its individual members taken severally. This is the indispensable condition of their social unity. If the whole system is, in any sense, higher or more valuable than its individual members, it is because it includes these without in any way impairing or diminishing their distinct individuality."[1] My *knowledge* of other minds, my *interest* in them, does, indeed, constitute part of my own being. But the other minds do not, therefore, enter

[1] G. F. Stout, *Proceedings of Aristotelian Society*, N.S. vol. xviii, 1918, p. 543.

into my being in any other manner or in any other respect.

The essential characteristic of a self-conscious individual is that it exists not simply for others, but for itself. Its true being is not merely what it is for another mind that knows it, but what it is for itself. There is no such thing as the 'confluence' or 'overlapping' of selves as existents. A self may be aware of contents largely identical with those of which another self is aware, but to speak as if their common contents in any way affected their essential distinctness betrays, it seems to me, the victim of a confusion. Uniqueness belongs to the very essence of a self-conscious individual. No one can ever, literally, or directly, see the world through another's eyes. That being so, it follows—I should say inevitably—that it is meaningless to speak of one consciousness as 'included' in another, or to speak of a Mind that 'includes all minds', and of a man as, in such sense 'a part of God'. What holds good in this respect of finite consciousnesses must also be true of a divine Mind, so far as the divine Mind is conceived as an *existing* self-consciousness. If, then, we are to think of God as a self-conscious being, the element of otherness must remain; the experiences of finite selves cannot form part of the divine experience in the same sense, or in any other sense, in which they are the experiences of the selves in question. The supreme Spirit may know what those experiences are, may even, if you like, know them 'from the inside', may have Himself similar experiences, but a finite mind's experience cannot be His experience, nor part of it.[1]

[1] Cf. *supra*, pp. 144–145.

7. A similar line of argument would lead, I think, to the conclusion that a 'universal Self-consciousness', if by that be meant an actually existent reality, is a contradiction in terms. Any self-conscious mind that exists must, as an *existent*, be concrete and individual, and equally so whether the mind in question be the mind of man or the mind of God. As an existent reality, God must be one of many existents; His existence cannot *be* the existence of others, nor the existence of others His. To meet this contention with the easy retort that it allows us but a finite God is surely to play with the ambiguity of terms. 'Infinity' is a slippery notion, and is susceptible of varied meanings. 'Infinite' in the sense of being that besides which and beyond which nothing else can exist, a divine consciousness, it is true, can never be. The totality of things, or what philosophers name the Absolute, cannot be identified with God, so long as God is conceived as a self-conscious Being. What philosophers designate the 'Absolute' must include God and other minds, the world of nature and the world of values, not indeed as isolated and disconnected entities, but rather as intimately related to one another and more especially to God, and as thus forming a system or coherent unity. If, then, by 'infinite' be meant 'the Absolute', God is not infinite. A quantitative whole of Reality, or one Reality that includes everything, would, no doubt, be 'infinite' in the sense of mere bigness or immeasurable magnitude; 'infinite' in the sense of being qualitatively perfect and complete it need not, and I should say, would not be. But it is 'infinity', I take it, in the latter sense that religion is concerned to

ascribe to God. The heaping of Pelion upon Ossa may mystify and bewilder; as an incentive to devotion it is powerless. Christian reflexion has made us familiar with the conception of the infinite worth and value of an individual soul. And from that conception there is here light to be won. For it suggests an 'infinity' very different from that of mere vastness. The infinitude of knowledge and of love has nothing in common with the endlessness of space. To know or to love anything or anyone genuinely or intensely *is* to be 'infinite' in regard to that person or thing. The mind of Peter Bell was limited and imperfect not because it was other than the primrose, but because it failed to appreciate the primrose; the poet was free from that limitation, not because the primrose was in any sense part of him, but because he could appropriate its beauty and experience the joy of such appropriation. And, so likewise, in regard to the world, God may be 'infinite', not because He *is* the world, nor because the world is part of Him; but because in and through Him the world has meaning and significance; because His knowledge of it is complete, and His solicitude for it perfect. To me, at all events, it seems simply a misuse of language to call an individual finite or limited *merely* because there are other individuals distinct from himself. If there were no other individuals, then his being would, indeed, be impoverished and his sphere of influence confined.

8. Unless I gravely err, the issue which in this lecture we have been considering is destined to be the issue that will be forced more and more upon the reflexion of thoughtful minds in the coming time. In

the later half of the Victorian era we were confronted with a materialism according to which the basis of the universe of existence was matter; and thought, feeling, consciousness of every kind, merely a by-product or concomitant of certain material processes. To that view no serious thinker of the present day would give his countenance, nor can it ever be resuscitated as a tenable philosophic theory. In the field of physical science itself the conception of a vast complex of material elements as the ultimate reality of the world of nature and of life has been definitely abandoned, and is clearly seen to be utterly insufficient to render intelligible even the physical events going on around us. The physicist is finding himself confronted with problems which half a century ago had not been so much as formulated. "Mind", says Sir James Jeans, "no longer appears as an accidental intruder into the realm of matter; we are beginning to suspect that we ought rather to hail it as the creator and governor of the realm of matter,—not, of course, our individual minds, but the mind in which the atoms out of which our individual minds have grown exist as thoughts." I confess I am not at all clear as to the way in which this statement should be interpreted. Many of Sir James Jeans's utterances would seem to indicate that he is intending to inculcate a theistic view of the universe not essentially different from that which I have been trying to unfold. But, in the passage just quoted, he would appear to be reaching forward to a pantheism more or less of the type we have just been discussing. I am not saying that the latter way of thinking is altogether devoid of attractiveness, or that it may not yield to many minds what seems to be a satisfactory solution of the problems of philosophy. But it is well to see clearly where the roads divide. Religious trust and aspiration are justified on the one basis; they can derive, so far as I can see, little sustenance from the other. Religion, in its highest form, rests, as I conceive it, upon belief in a supreme living and personal Mind; it loses its meaning if the ultimate ground of things be taken to be a system of thought-contents which preserve their timeless being while human souls, such as these are then supposed to be, arise and pass away.

INDEX